T0316596

Cambridge Elements ≡

Elements in Eighteenth-Century Connections
edited by
Eve Tavor Bannet
University of Oklahoma

SCIENCE AND READING IN THE EIGHTEENTH CENTURY

The Hardwicke Circle and the Royal Society, 1740–1766

Markman Ellis
Queen Mary University of London

CAMBRIDGE
UNIVERSITY PRESS

Shaftesbury Road, Cambridge CB2 8EA, United Kingdom

One Liberty Plaza, 20th Floor, New York, NY 10006, USA

477 Williamstown Road, Port Melbourne, VIC 3207, Australia

314–321, 3rd Floor, Plot 3, Splendor Forum, Jasola District Centre,
New Delhi – 110025, India

103 Penang Road, #05–06/07, Visioncrest Commercial, Singapore 238467

Cambridge University Press is part of Cambridge University Press & Assessment,
a department of the University of Cambridge.

We share the University's mission to contribute to society through the pursuit of
education, learning and research at the highest international levels of excellence.

www.cambridge.org
Information on this title: www.cambridge.org/9781009217200

DOI: 10.1017/9781009217217

First published 2023

A catalogue record for this publication is available from the British Library.

Additional resources for this publication at www.cambridge.org/scienceandreading

ISBN 978-1-009-21720-0 Paperback
ISSN 2632-5578 (online)
ISSN 2632-556X (print)

Science and Reading in the Eighteenth Century

The Hardwicke Circle and the Royal Society, 1740–1766

Elements in Eighteenth-Century Connections

DOI: 10.1017/9781009217217
First published online: February 2023

Markman Ellis
Queen Mary University of London

Author for correspondence: Markman Ellis, m.ellis@qmul.ac.uk

Abstract: *Science and Reading in the Eighteenth Century* studies the reading habits of a group of historians and science administrators known as the Hardwicke Circle. The research is based on an analysis of the reading recorded in the 'Weekly Letter', an unpublished private correspondence written from 1741 to 1766 between Thomas Birch (1705–66), Secretary of the Royal Society, and Philip Yorke (1720–90), later second earl of Hardwicke. Birch and Yorke were omnivorous, voracious and active readers. The analysis uses the Weekly Letter to quantify the texts with which they engaged and explores the role of reading in their intellectual life. The research argues that this evidence shows that, in the early 1750s, the Hardwicke Circle pivoted from a focus on early modern British history to a new concern with the reform and renovation of British intellectual institutions, especially the Royal Society.

Keywords: reading, science, Thomas Birch, Hardwicke Circle, Royal Society

ISBNs: 9781009217200 (PB), 9781009217217 (OC)
ISSNs: 2632-5578 (online), 2632-556X (print)

Contents

Introduction: Reading History and the Royal Society

Does the intellectual hinterland of men of science matter? It is accepted that natural philosophers will master technical practices and processes associated with their science: an astronomer will be adept at the workings both of a telescope and of the mathematics needed to analyse and present their results, just as a botanist will be familiar with the collecting, pressing and presentational practices of a herbarium. Should reading also be included in the technical practices expected of a natural philosopher? What do we know about the reading of natural philosophers in the eighteenth century, and how does that reading contribute to the history of science?

This Element explores the reading habits of the Hardwicke Circle, a small group of men influential in the Royal Society, and its primary publication, *Philosophical Transactions*, in the mid-eighteenth century. The principal actors are Thomas Birch (1705–66), Secretary of the Royal Society from 1752 to 1765, and Philip Yorke (1720–90), second earl of Hardwicke from 1764. It explores and measures the reading undertaken by these men and asks what books and manuscripts, and the cultural practices they supported, meant to them. They were voracious and omnivorous readers and, while some of their reading was undertaken 'merely' for entertainment or curiosity, they also developed a range of more studious reading practices that allowed them to survey, identify, catalogue and summarise their reading. In their hands, the practice of reading was an active and productive pursuit closely integrated into their wider intellectual culture. Unusually, perhaps, they left an organised and systematic record of their reading in their correspondence. In their letters, they not only gave notice of the texts they read and encountered; they also performed a range of scholarly and critical activities, including attribution and correction and, sometimes at heroic scale, summarisation and transcription. They also searched for texts for each other, purchased, borrowed or lent them, and sent them between their houses. Considered together, these practices amount to a distinctive Hardwicke Circle reading culture.

This Element argues that Hardwicke Circle reading practices had been established in the course of their engagement with history writing, both the writing and publication of their own works of history, but also in managing the print and manuscript resources needed for that writing. They made use of these organised and studious reading habits to measure and determine the value of their own history writing and that of their historiographical allies, critics and enemies. The power and privilege that accrued to Yorke through the influence of his father, Philip Yorke, Lord Chancellor Hardwicke (1690–1764), facilitated the dominance of his circle in the Royal Society in the 1750s.[1] Their systems and practices of reading, the Hardwicke Circle reading culture, were subsequently deployed in processes that organised and categorised their reading in natural philosophy, especially learned journals and the publications of scientific institutions. Analysis of their reading allows us to track their pivot from history writing to scientific administration in the 1750s as they worked to reform and renovate the back-office functions of the Royal Society and the British Museum.

To investigate the reading cultures of the Hardwicke Circle, this Element makes a quantitative study of the evidence of their reading recorded in the 'Weekly Letter', a private correspondence written between Birch and Yorke from 1741 to 1766. It comprises 687 letters in total, 433 of which were written by Birch, together with 254 replies by Yorke (British Library: Add MS 35396–400).[2] Birch described his correspondence as a report on 'the State of the Literary World' and that of 'the Political one'.[3] Sent on Saturday, Birch's contribution consisted of a remarkably regular weekly letter – or hebdomadal – describing the political, literary and scientific news of London. It was written on a half-folio sheet folded in two to create a four-page letter, occasionally extended by another bifolium to make a more substantial letter of five or six pages. Birch's notebooks show that his contribution was carefully composed and revised and that the sent letter was a fine copy.[4] Yorke's replies, describing his literary, political and scientific responses, were less frequent, less regular, shorter and more off-hand, reflecting his more elevated status. Although a late example, the Weekly Letter adopts and imitates many of the practices of the seventeenth-century scribal newsletter, a media format that was the subject of Birch and Yorke's own research.[5]

The research presented here analyses the Weekly Letter for evidence of the Hardwicke Circle's reading culture. It identifies the texts they engaged with and explores the role of reading in their intellectual life by quantifying and analysing them according to distinct criteria. The research takes an expansive view of reading so as to include all forms of reading matter, including pamphlets,

---

[1] For clarity, this research refers to Philip Yorke, second earl of Hardwicke (1720–90), as Yorke, and his father the Lord Chancellor, Philip Yorke, first earl of Hardwicke (1690–1764), as Hardwicke.

[2] British Library [hereafter BL]: Add MS 35396–400: Correspondence of Philip Yorke, second earl of Hardwicke, with Rev. Thomas Birch, D. D., Secretary to the Royal Society; Gunther, *Birch*, pp. 45–6.

[3] BL: Add MS 35396: Birch to Yorke, 29 August 1741, ff. 13–14 (14v). All Birch letters addressed from London unless otherwise noted.

[4] BL: Add MS 4471: Private Accompt Books 1759–61, ff. 143–56.

[5] On the organisation of the Weekly Letter see Ellis, 'Birch's "Weekly letter"'. On the scribal newsletter or *nouvelle à la main* see Moureau, *Répertoire des nouvelles à main*.

manuscripts and other written intellectual products (reports, sermons and letters), some of which were read aloud, as well as the ephemeral or quotidian world of newspapers, journals and periodicals, all of which were embedded within a series of events and assemblies such as lectures, meetings, performances and dinners. The research also explores books that circulated between Birch and Yorke and their wider circle; their antiquarian interests in seventeenth-century English, British and Irish history; and their curiosity about contemporary publication practices. It situates these reading events in the intellectual and political interests of the Hardwicke Circle and the Royal Society.[6]

The term 'reading' in this Element is inclusive and extended. Recent approaches to reading studies have expanded our conception of reading from the passive consumption of written material, to seeing it as an active process, encompassing a wide range of things to do with books, as Leah Price memorably phrased it. In her study, Price set out to 'reconstruct nineteenth-century understandings of, and feelings toward, the uses of printed matter'. She establishes three 'operations' that happen to books: 'reading (doing something with words), handling (doing something with the object), and circulating (doing something to, or with, other persons by means of the book – whether by cementing or severing relationships, whether by giving and receiving books or by withholding and rejecting them'.[7] Without describing these three modes in exactly the same way, Abigail Williams's *The Social Life of Books* (2017) further explores the diverse ways that books in the eighteenth century were the subject of collective and sociable activities, including reading clubs, reading aloud, circulating libraries and common-placing. There are some distinctive features of the Birch and Yorke reading, such as their sustained interest in reading beyond the printed book, especially manuscript, often in extensive and unpublished historical manuscript collections; and the forms of reading aloud practised at the Royal Society.

Historians of reading have described the middle of the eighteenth century as an important point of transition. An influential distinction has been drawn between intensive and extensive reading, as Rolf Engelsing was the first to argue in 1970.[8] Intensive readers read and reread a few texts, 'slowly, repeatedly, reverently', such as the Bible or Livy, books that never become outdated or irrelevant to their readers. In Engelsing's view, the latter was giving way

---

[6] The term 'Hardwicke Circle' was not used in the eighteenth century. It was first used in Higson, 'Lord Willoughby of Parham', p. 172, and gained currency in Miller's 'The "Hardwicke Circle"', pp. 74–81.

[7] Price, *How to do things with books*, pp. 5–6.

[8] Engelsing, 'Die perioden'; Wittmann, 'Reading revolution'.

increasingly to the former in the eighteenth century. Birch and Yorke read in both these modes, depending on the context. Robert DeMaria's *Samuel Johnson and the Life of Reading* elaborates four modes of reading – 'study', 'perusal', 'mere reading' and 'curious reading' – the first two of which might be mapped on to Engelsing's intensive, and the latter two, extensive reading. Birch and Yorke certainly undertook reading in the mode DeMaria calls 'study' (repeated, learned and in depth) and 'perusal' (more gentlemanly, immediate and improving), although, like Johnson, Yorke was sometimes reluctant to be seen as too studious and pedantic. Birch's notekeeping, summarisation and transcription habits are part of this kind of the practice of scholarly study. Equally, Birch and Yorke enjoyed the quotidian pleasures of periodicals, novels, satire and literary gossip – forms of 'mere' and 'curious' reading, consuming many texts and books, encountered in diverse ways and consumed by 'skimming and skipping, devouring and discarding'.[9] Although DeMaria's study of Johnson's reading as a man of letters is significant, the Hardwicke Circle's reading culture remains distinctive, especially in its preference for scholarly systems and practices.

This Element begins with a prosopographical account of the key players, especially Birch and Yorke, and describes the role the Weekly Letter played in the Hardwicke Circle. It scopes the dimensions of the Hardwicke Circle and surveys its successful effort to gain control of the Royal Society's higher offices in the early 1750s. Section 2 undertakes a detailed analysis of the Birch-Yorke Weekly Letter in a five-year sample period from 1750 to 1754. In this period, the correspondents exchanged 139 letters (93 from Birch, 46 from Yorke). Adopting a quantitative approach, it begins by detailing the parameters of the sample, defining key terms such as 'reading event' and exploring important caveats about the data. Section 3 anatomises the distinctive activities of Birch and Yorke's reading practices, including noticing, attributing, requesting and summarising. Section 4 explores in more detail their engagement with literature, philosophy and history, using a case study approach to explore some topics in more detail, which is extended in Section 5 to science publications and related activities, especially the distinctive Royal Society practice of reading aloud. The final section explores comparative data derived from analogous reading circles in Britain in broadly the same period and undertakes a discussion of how reading in the Hardwicke Circle helps to understand their pivot from history to scientific administration.

---

[9] Price, 'Reading: the state of the discipline', p. 317.

Figure 1 James Wills, 'Thomas Birch (1705–1766) Secretary 1752–1765', 1737, oil on canvas, Royal Society of London, P/0008

1 The Hardwicke Circle and the Royal Society

Thomas Birch was born a Quaker and the son of a coffee mill maker in 1705 in Clerkenwell, London. He was educated in Quaker schools, including that of Josiah Welby at Turnbull Street, Clerkenwell, where he also subsequently taught as an usher.[10] After the death of his wife and son in 1729, Birch was baptised into the Anglican Church in 1730 and ordained in 1731. Birch was appointed one of three chief editors of the ten-volume English edition of Bayle's *General Dictionary, Historical and Critical* that appeared between 1734 and 1741, for which Birch completed more than six hundred new biographies. For this he was elected a Fellow of the Royal Society in February 1735, although his nomination also noted he was 'A Gentleman well versed in Mathematicks and Natural Philosophy' (Figure 1).[11] Having come to the attention of Philip Yorke's father, the attorney-general Sir Philip Yorke, he was presented to the

---

[10] BL: Add MS 4268: Andrew Ducarel, 'Notes about the late Dr. Tho. Birch', f. 1r–v.
[11] Royal Society EC/1734/25.

vicarage of Ulting in Essex in 1732, the first of a series of preferments that culminated in a wealthy city parish, the Rectory of St Margaret Pattens, in 1746. These church preferments gave Birch time to pursue his literary and historical projects.[12]

Birch published a series of well-respected and very substantial works of history in the 1740s, including *The State Papers of John Thurloe, Esq.* in seven folio volumes in 1742; the lavishly illustrated *The Heads of Illustrious Persons of Great Britain* (1743–51); *The Life of the Honourable Robert Boyle* in 1744; and *An Historical View of the Negotiations between the Courts of England, France, and Brussels, from the year 1592 to 1617* in 1749. His *Memoirs of the Reign of Queen Elizabeth* (1754) and *The History of the Royal Society of London* (1756–7) are discussed in Section 4. Having demonstrated his administrative skills as the treasurer of the Society for the Encouragement of Learning from 1736 to 1738, Birch rose to prominence in a series of metropolitan intellectual institutions. He was a director of the Society of Antiquaries from 1736 to 1747, with oversight of the institution's publications, Secretary of the Royal Society from 1752, and a Founding Trustee of the British Museum when it was established in 1753. Through these appointments and his own activities, Birch was unusually well connected in the world of learning, especially among printers and booksellers, men of science, historian clergy and the writers of *belles lettres*.

Philip Yorke was educated at Newcome's school in Hackney and proceeded to Corpus Christi College, Cambridge, in 1737. Yorke had literary ambitions, especially in the sphere of gentlemanly satire and history writing. Yorke introduced Birch to his Cambridge scholar-friends in 1740 and immediately pressed him to serve as a kind of literary agent in London. Birch's bibliographical services included research, advice about publication and proof correction. He also searched for, acquired and borrowed books and manuscripts for Yorke. Birch assisted with Yorke's first publication, a gently ironic historical essay on Roman news entitled 'On the *Acta Diurna* of the *Old Romans*' which appeared in *Gentleman's Magazine* in early 1741. Birch also worked on *Athenian Letters* (1741–3), a collaborative fiction mostly written by Philip and his younger brother Charles Yorke, but with writing contributions from least ten others, including Birch. It anachronistically repurposed the form of the scribal newsletter to relate the history of the Peloponnesian War between Greece and Sparta in the fifth century BC, as recorded by Thucydides and Plutarch. *Athenian Letters* was printed but not published in an edition of twelve copies, one for each of the contributors, in four volumes in 1741 and 1743. By August 1741,

---

[12] See Gunther, *Birch*, and Miller, 'Birch', *Oxford dictionary of national biography* (*ODNB*).

Figure 2 Allan Ramsay, 'The Honble. Philip Yorke Eldest Son of the Right Honble. Philip Lord High Chancellor of Great Britain married Ano. 1740 to Jemima Marchioness Great Daughter of John Lord Glenorchy', 1741, oil painting on canvas, National Trust Wimpole

when Birch inaugurated the Weekly Letter, he was closely engaged in the Yorke household's literary and intellectual life. When Yorke was in London, on Monday mornings Birch regularly attended breakfast with Yorke at his townhouse in St James's Square; when he was at Wrest, Birch maintained contact through the Weekly Letter and made an annual visit.[13]

Yorke's personal inclinations, together with an awareness of the propriety of his father's Hardwicke name, inclined him to eschew the public life of the writer in favour of a private life as a scholar and historian (Figure 2). His father had negotiated for him a very lucrative sinecure in the Exchequer. Yorke left Cambridge without completing his degree when, on 23 May 1740, he married Lady Jemima Campbell (1722–97), *suo jure* Marchioness Grey (hereafter referred to as Lady Grey (Figure 3)). The granddaughter of the Duke of Kent,

---

[13] The Birch-Yorke relationship is described as 'friendship as intermediation' in Schellenberg, *Literary coteries*, pp. 25–59, and as a friendship mediated by patronage by Almagor, 'Friendship', 468–97.

Figure 3 Allan Ramsay, 'Jemima Marchioness Grey Daughter of John Lord Glenorchy married Ano. 1740 to the Honble. Philip Yorke Eldest Son of the Right Honble. Philip Lord Hardwicke Lord High Chancellor of Great Britain', 1741, oil painting on canvas, National Trust Wimpole

her inherited property included Wrest Park, a substantial country house near Flitwick in Bedfordshire. Yorke and Lady Grey had an affectionate marriage, sharing interests in landscape gardening, architecture, natural philosophy and literature. Yorke was elected a Fellow of the Royal Society in January 1741; and then to the House of Commons for Reigate, Surrey, in 1741; and in 1747, for Cambridgeshire.

Both Birch and Yorke benefitted from the political and financial power of Yorke's father, Philip Yorke, the first earl of Hardwicke (Figure 4). Trained as a barrister, he was elected a Member of Parliament in 1719 and was appointed attorney-general in 1724. In 1725, he purchased the estate of Hardwicke in Gloucestershire for £24,000, and, in 1740, that of Wimpole in Cambridgeshire for £100,000. Sir Robert Walpole appointed him Lord Chancellor in 1737,

Figure 4 John Wills, engraved by James McArdell, 'The Right Honble. Philip Lord Hardwicke, Baron of Hardwicke, Lord High Chancellor of Great Britain', 1744–54, engraving, Rijksmuseumn Amsterdam, RP-P-OB-32.445

a post he occupied until 1756. He was created first earl of Hardwicke in 1754. As well as being a powerful and active judge, he was a politician of great ability affiliated with the Court Whigs as the Duke of Newcastle's most trusted advisor. Hardwicke's post as Lord Chancellor made him, as the chief law lord, a man capable of considerable patronage and largesse. He was very concerned to advance the interests of his children. As Horace Walpole said of the Yorkes in September 1757: 'That family is very powerful.'[14] Birch and Yorke channelled his influence to their own local and institutional purposes in the Hardwicke Circle. In so doing they promoted the cultural programme of the Court Whigs: firmly supporting the Hanoverian succession, the rule of law, constitutional monarchy in the model of 1688, orthodox Protestant and Anglican theology, the

---

[14] Horace Walpole to Horace Mann, 3 September 1757, *Walpole's correspondence*, Vol. 21, p. 129.

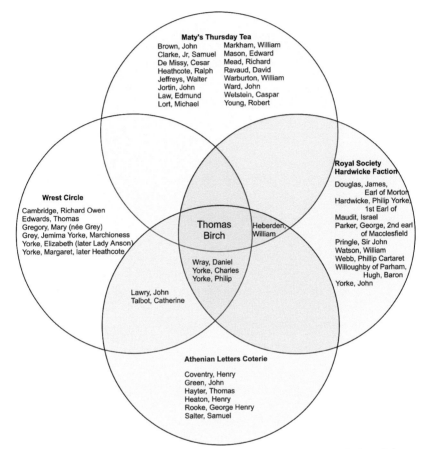

Figure 5 The Hardwicke Circle, 1740–66

value of trade, credit and the commercial system; and a distrust of popular democracy, riots and mobs, sexual libertinage, Catholic superstition and Jacobite revisionism.[15]

The Weekly Letter, written by Birch and Yorke, was an important conduit of information for the Hardwicke Circle in the Royal Society. Birch and Yorke's letters operated as the mediating connection between a series of overlapping but discontinuous social circles and intellectual networks, as shown in Figure 5. As the only point of contact between these circles and networks, Birch acts as

---

[15] Browning, *The court Whigs*, pp. 151–74.

a 'social broker' in the sense defined by Ronald Burt to describe a person that bridges otherwise unconnected networks and, by controlling the flow of information and resources between them, augments their own social capital.[16] The Weekly Letter exists in the gaps between geographically and socially distinct networks in which Birch and Yorke participated. Yorke's domestic circle was focussed on his home at Wrest and included Jemima Lady Grey, her aunt Mary Gregory (1719–61) and the author Catherine Talbot (1721–70). Four of Yorke's five siblings were frequent visitors, especially the lawyer Charles (FRS, 1722–70); Elizabeth Yorke, later Lady Anson (1725–60); John Yorke (FRS, 1728–1801); and Margaret Yorke, later Heathcote (1733–69). Yorke's brother Joseph (1724–92), a diplomat and soldier created Baron Dover in 1788, was abroad for most of these decades but maintained a steady correspondence from The Hague and Paris. Yorke's Cambridge associates, brought together by *Athenian Letters*, remained close intellectual associates, especially Rev. John Lawry (FRS, 1714–77) and Daniel Wray (FRS, 1701–83). To these Yorke circles, in which he participated as an invited guest, Birch also brought his own circle of London philosophers, who assembled to drink tea at Maty's Thursday Tea. Birch's own correspondence was very wide but, in the 1750s, his most frequent and regular correspondents, as preserved in the twenty-four volumes of his correspondence (BL: Add MS 4300–23), were primarily men of two kinds: a group of fellow clergy, often known for their controversial views, like Rev. Henry Etough and Rev. John Jones; and a group of Fellows of the Royal Society, especially John Ward, Professor of Rhetoric at Gresham College and George Parker, second earl of Macclesfield, who was elected President of the Royal Society in 1752 with the support of the Hardwicke Circle.[17]

The Weekly Letter between Birch and Yorke imagined Birch located in London at his house in Great Norfolk Street, off the Strand, in a book-strewn study and library (Figure 6). Birch's house was an urban rectory, but as

---

[16] Burt, *Brokerage and closure*, 25–6.

[17] BL: Add MS 4300–23: Collection of letters addressed to Thomas Birch; 1726–66. The collection was arranged by Birch and the letters were selected by him using unknown criteria. These volumes exclude letters from the Yorke family (in BL: Add MS 4325). The ten most frequent correspondents in the 1750s are Rev. Henry Etough (1697–1757), Rector of Therfield, Hertfordshire (44 letters); Rev. John Jones (1700–70), Curate of Welwyn Hertfordshire (42); Rev. Josiah Tucker, DD (1713–99) Dean of Gloucester (40); John Ward, LLD (1679?–1758), Professor of Rhetoric at Gresham College, FRS (28); George Parker, second earl of Macclesfield (1697–1764), President of the Royal Society (28); Rev. John Orr (fl. 1739–72), Archdeacon of Ferns, Ireland (27); Johann Caspar Wetstein (1695–1760) Rector of Helmingham, FRS (25); Rev. William Murdin (1703–60), Vicar of Shalford (24); Bishop Charles Lyttelton, DD (1714–68), Bishop of Carlisle, FRS (19); Rev. Stephen Hales, DD (1677–1761), Rector of Porlock, Somerset, FRS (18). With thanks to Stephanie Howard-Smith.

Figure 6 Letter Cover, Philip Yorke to Thomas Birch, 19 July 1753, Add MS 35398, f. 135v. © The British Library Board.

constructed in the letters, was closely networked with booksellers' shops, learned institutions, libraries, secondhand book markets, book auctions, not to mention coffeehouses, dining clubs, theatres and other sources of information, including of course the institutions of learned London such as the Royal Society. Meanwhile, the letter imagined Yorke at Wrest Park, his country estate; specifically in his private study, accessible only to him, or perhaps in his library, accessible to the family and guests. Wrest was a country house inhabited by Yorke's family circle (Lady Grey, their children) and many visitors. The regular group, identified as 'the Wrest circle' by Jemima Hubberstey, included Philip's younger siblings (the lawyer Charles Yorke (FRS), the army officer James Yorke, John Yorke (FRS) and Elizabeth Lady Anson); gentleman scholars such as Daniel Wray (FRS) and the poet Thomas Edwards, as well as Catherine Talbot and Margaret Grey, amongst others.[18] Both Birch and Yorke make use of the imaginary of the 'study', a space in the house in which books and papers are lost and found, and the 'library' – in Yorke's case, a distinct architectural space as well as a collection of books. Yorke eulogised the library

---

[18]   Hubberstey, 'The Wrest circle'.

at Wrest for its cosy peacefulness, praising how 'the Library Fire in the Evening enlivens both Study & Conversation'.[19] Inviting Birch in 1750 to make his regular summer visit, Yorke said, 'The great Chair & Library fire shall be ready for you.'[20]

The Weekly Letter, sent between Great Norfolk Street and Wrest, was the conduit between the working world of Enlightenment London and the Hardwicke family with its political patronage and great wealth. Birch's world included coffeehouses, especially the intellectual ones like Tom's Devereux Court, Rawthmell's Coffee House on St Martin's Lane, and Lloyd's Coffee-House near the Exchange. He was also well acquainted with booksellers' shops and printing shops, the Inns of Court and the London palaces of bishops and archbishops. Birch's London also included sociable spaces such as Maty's Tea and the Royal Society Dining Club at the Mitre Tavern. Maty's Thursday Tea was an important unofficial channel for the exchange of information and gossip between scientific, theological and literary circles. In June 1751, the Huguenot physician and writer Matthew Maty invited Birch to 'come and drink tea at my house' with the historian Dr John Jortin. This tradition continued nearly every week until Birch's death in 1766, at various houses and on various days. Birch was also a stalwart member of the dining club that met after Royal Society meetings at the Mitre Tavern, sometimes supplied with venison from Yorke estates.[21]

Figure 7 visualises the flows of knowledge in the Birch-Yorke informa-tion network. Despite their geographical proximity, the social and cultural gap between Birch and Yorke was considerable. Birch inhabited the world of scholars, divines, writers and booksellers, the republic of letters; Yorke, as a Member of Parliament and the son of the Lord Chancellor, that of the corridors of power and influence. Birch and Yorke, meeting in the Weekly Letter, along with others such as Daniel Wray and Matthew Maty, function as intermediaries or brokers between these worlds, creating in their corres-pondence a language and venue for knowledge exchange.[22] Many of Birch's habitual spaces in literary London were virtually inaccessible to Yorke, even when he was present in London, as his elite status would have vitiated the potential for sociable equality and free exchange. Equally, Yorke's access to financial influence and political power gave him a kind of political capital and influence.

---

[19] BL: Add MS 35398: Yorke to Birch, Wrest, 21 October 1755, ff. 299–300 (299r).
[20] BL: Add MS 35397: Yorke to Birch, Wrest, 11 October 1750, ff. 302–3 (303r).
[21] Birch was a member of the dining club from its foundation in 1743: Royal Society, GB 0117 RSC. See also Geikie, *Annals,* and Allibone, *Dining clubs.*
[22] Schaffer et al., *Brokered world.*

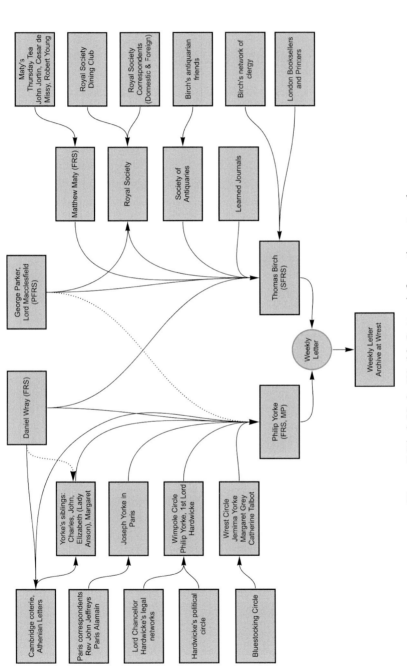

Figure 7 Birch-Yorke Weekly Letter: information network

The Royal Society and the Hardwicke Coup

Birch and Yorke operated their Hardwicke influence in a period that is known in the historiography of the Royal Society as a time of decline. David Miller has characterised the middle decades of the eighteenth century, between the presidencies of Isaac Newton and Joseph Banks, as the 'Valley of Darkness'.[23] This understanding of this period emerged in the nineteenth century, when commentators and reformers of the Royal Society, looking back at its history, contrasted the Society in the mid-eighteenth century with the vibrant first decades of the Society in the Restoration. They found further evidence of the Society's decline in the mid-eighteenth century in the attacks launched upon it by satirists, and in deprecatory comments written by travellers and observers – forms of writing that they were collecting and collating for the first time.[24] The eighteenth-century satirist-critics in particular, they concluded, opined that the Royal Society was little more than a talking shop for aristocratic *dilletantes* who showed an excessive appetite for accounts of wonders submitted by credulous rural clergy and little interest in the actual work of natural philosophy.

The declinist narrative has been shown to be somewhat overstated in recent decades. Richard Sorrenson has demonstrated that the Royal Society steadily increased the number of its fellows, its income and its capital through the eighteenth century. He has further argued that the social background of its fellows remained largely consistent and that its publications, especially the *Philosophical Transactions*, remained focussed on empirical studies and mixed mathematics.[25] He has contended that satirists' attacks on the Royal Society were often motivated by particular ad hominem causes and cannot be read as uncomplicated and accurate assessments of the institution. Nonetheless, the critical comments by satirists and foreign visitors, as well as some fellows, created an air of crisis around the Royal Society and its leadership at the beginning of the 1750s. During Martin Folkes's presidency (1741–52), complaints about the administration increased (Figure 8). Henry Lyons reports 'the average number of Council meetings in each year fell from seven to five' and 'the Ordinary meetings had now more of a literary than a scientific character'.[26] When the Hardwicke Circle took control of the Royal Society's administration in the early 1750s, they did so as reformers of its institutional processes and its principal publication, *Philosophical Transactions*.

Birch, a Fellow since 1735, flourished in the Royal Society in the 1740s, both in their official meetings and also its ancillary sociability. In the middle of the

---

[23] Miller, '"Valley of Darkness"', pp. 155–66.
[24] Thomson, *History of the Royal Society*, p. 12. [25] Sorrenson, *Perfect mechanics*.
[26] Lyons, 'Officers', p. 128.

Figure 8 James McArdell, after Thomas Hudson, 'Martin Folkes Esqr. President of the Royal Society', 1741–54, engraving, Rijksmuseumn Amsterdam, RP-P-OB-32.41

eighteenth century, about one third of the fellowship were 'Working' or 'Physical' Fellows, elected for their abilities and achievements in natural philosophy, and two thirds were 'literary' or 'honorary', elected for their antiquarian or historical work and writing, like Birch, or simply their noble status and connections. Terms like these, drawn from comments by Emanuel Mendes da Costa (FRS), are of course imprecise and problematic, but elections of the officers of the society to the Council inevitably resolved to such factional identities, although in fact many candidates blurred such differences.[27] Folkes, elected in 1741, had literary and archaeological interests while his Secretaries were an astronomer, Peter Daval (from 1747), and a physician, Dr Cromwell Mortimer (from 1730).[28]

---

[27] BL: Add MS 28535: Emanuel Mendes da Costa to William Borlase (FRS), 27 February 1752, ff. 70–3 (72r).

[28] Lyons, 'Officers', p. 128.

At the anniversary meeting in November 1749, Birch was elected to the Council for 1750, and again, in 1751, for 1752, as was Yorke's friend, the antiquary Daniel Wray.[29] The opportunity for further advance of Birch presented itself soon after, when Mortimer died in January 1752. Birch competed for the post against Dr Gowin Knight (1713–72), a physician with a solid research record on magnetism and the magnetic compass who had been awarded the prestigious Copley Medal in 1747. Gowin's cause was promoted by the 'Working' or 'Physical' party while Birch's supporters were mostly drawn from the literary and honorary members. Birch won by ninety-one votes to seventy-two: in his *Diary* Birch celebrated the event with the laconic comment, 'Electus sum Secretarius Regia Societatis'.[30] Birch was at work as Secretary of the Royal Society from 25 January 1752, alongside Peter Davall, both paid sixty pounds per annum with a gratuity of ten guineas. One of his first tasks was to write up the Royal Society minutes in the Journal Book from 5 December 1751.[31]

By late 1751, Folkes was in ill health. Birch later said he had been 'seiz'd with a Palsy' which paralysed his left side.[32] William Stukeley (FRS) described it as a 'paralytick stroke'.[33] In summer 1752, Birch realised that Folkes's ill health had rendered him incapable of resuming his duties as president. In the Weekly Letter for 14 October 1752, Birch described his state of health: 'Our President, whom I visited yesterday complains greatly of a Cold which affected him in such a manner yesterday sennight with a convulsive Cough, that he was thought actually expiring, & this Cough still returns frequently, tho' in a less Degree.'[34]

Birch saw this report in a dynastic light: 'He gives no intimation of any Desire to be discharg'd from the Office which he is never likely to be again capable of executing; and we are unwilling to take any step this year that may possibly hurt him.'[35] As Birch saw it, it was not possible to remove the president against his will, even when he was manifestly incapacitated. Before the annual meeting Folkes indicated he would resign (he had a second stroke on 25 June 1754 and died three days later). The front-runner for the contest for the presidency was Lord Charles Cavendish (1704–83),

---

[29] BL: Add MS 4478C: Birch Diary, 1750, ff. 171, 172; 1751 30 November, f. 203. Royal Society, Journal Book Original: JBO/20, p. 574.

[30] BL: Add MS 4478C: Birch, Diary, 30 November 1751, f. 203.

[31] Royal Society: JBO/22, p. 1.

[32] BL: Add MS 4222: Thomas Birch, 'Memoirs of the life of Martin Folkes', ff. 30r–31v.

[33] Stukeley to Johnson, 24 April 1752, in Stukeley, *Correspondence*, p. 178; Roos, *Folkes*, pp. 341–3.

[34] BL: Add MS 35398: Birch to Yorke, 14 October 1752, ff. 104–5 (104r).

[35] BL: Add MS 35398: Birch to Yorke, 14 October 1752, ff. 104–5 (104r–v).

Figure 9 Thomas Hudson, 'Portrait of George Parker, 2nd Earl of Macclesfield
     (1697–1764)', 1754, oil on canvas. Royal Society RS-9663.12

distinguished in electrical research and a cousin by marriage to Jemima Yorke.
After Cavendish declined to pursue the office, a firm Hardwicke candidate,
George Parker, second earl of Macclesfield, came forward (Figure 9). Birch
reported in the Weekly Letter for 14 October 1752: 'When we proceed to
a new Choice, Lord Macclesfield will have no Competitor, for Lord Charles
Cavendish has lately declared to Mr. Watson his Resolution not to accept of
the Presidency.'[36]

At the election to Council that year, Yorke too was elected, serving
alongside Birch, Lord Willoughby of Parham, and Macclesfield, who was
elected the president unopposed. As an astronomer and mathematician of
high standing, Macclesfield might have been thought to belong with the
Working members. But he was very closely allied with the Hardwickes, with
whom he shared political allegiance in Parliament as a Court Whig. Between
1750 and 1752, he had worked closely with the Hardwickes, father and son,
and Lord Chesterfield to secure the passage of the bill to reform the

---

[36] BL: Add MS 35398: Birch to Yorke, 14 October 1752, ff. 104–5 (104v).

calendar.[37] With the election of Macclesfield, the Hardwicke Circle coup was complete.

2 The Weekly Letter Reading Database (WLRD)
2.1 Methodology

This section is focussed on the quantitative analysis of a five-year sample of the Weekly Letter from 1750 to 1754. This is an significant period for Birch and Yorke, during which the Hardwicke Circle complete their successful bid to control the Royal Society's administration. The aim of this analysis is to expand the understanding of Birch and Yorke's intellectual interests by studying their reading and encounters with books and other reading matter. To do this, the Weekly Letter in this period has been processed (analysed and read) to harvest data about books and reading, creating a comparatively small, discrete and highly curated data set.[38] As a humanities project operating at the intersection of the history of science, the history of the book and English studies, this involved at least three activities: (i) data analysis of primary texts, (ii) deployment of disciplinary knowledge to inform the metadata (iii) and acts of interpretation conducted through close reading and the methods of literary history.[39]

There are important caveats to recognise with the data. Although the Weekly Letter archive was meticulously curated and maintained by its authors at its formation and is complete in and of itself, it is nonetheless only a partial history of its principal agents' reading. The primary limit here is chronological and seasonal. The Weekly Letter was written when Yorke was out of London for the summer vacation. He left London soon after the start of the parliamentary recess, which was usually in May. He returned either when Parliament was recalled or for the anniversary meeting of the Royal Society on St Andrew's Day, 30 November, whichever was the sooner. For the rest of the year, Birch and Yorke used other methods to facilitate their mutual intellectual interests and discuss their reading. For example, Birch's diary records that they met face-to-face at breakfast on Mondays, usually with Lady Grey, and although books and reading remained a central topic of interest for them, those conversations left no written record. A further caveat is that the creation of the data set is based on judgements grounded in disciplinary knowledge about what constitutes a 'reading event'. For example, it draws a hard distinction between information

---

[37] Macclesfield, 'Solar and the lunar years'; *Act for regulating the commencement of the year 24 Geo.II.c.23.*

[38] On small data projects see Berman, *Principles of big data*, pp. xx–xxiii; Boyd, 'Critical questions for big data', p. 667.

[39] Kleinman, 'Small and unusual data'; Drucker, *Digital humanities coursebook.*

about literary or book-related material and the political 'news' in the Weekly
Letter: this boundary was of course fluid and 'news' of books, especially
political pamphlets, obviously functioned as both.

In the five 'seasons' of the Weekly Letter analysed here – 1750 to 1754 – the
correspondents exchanged 139 letters (93 from Birch, 46 from Yorke), as well
as a further 8 enclosures, as described in Table 1. These yield 842 'reading
event' data points spread relatively evenly over the five-year sample, with an
average of 6.1 data points in each letter. In this research, a 'reading event' is
defined as any discussion or mention of the reading of textual material, including printed books, pamphlets, tracts, maps, engraved prints, newspapers, periodicals, plays, poems, novels and print ephemera; manuscript letters, drafts and
transcriptions; and collections of manuscripts, letters and print, including whole
libraries. It also includes material that was read aloud and lectures at learned
institutions. 'Reading events' note each iteration of that event: each text in each
letter. Accordingly, the same text named in three different letters produces three
reading events while the same text named three times in one letter produces one.
A letter noting three different texts generates three reading events.

In the Weekly Letter Reading Database (WLRD), each reading event is
linked to an appropriate record: either to a printed text in the English Short
Title Catalogue, a relevant library catalogue entry in the case of manuscript
collections, or to other databases such as Burney Newspapers.[40] Subsequent
analysis explores a range of distinctive features of the data:

   (i)   dimensions of the case study reading sample 1750–4;
   (ii) type or kind of reading material (novel, history, satire, verse, tract etc.);
   (iii) media format of reading event item (book, pamphlet, periodical etc.);
   (iv) sustained readings (texts with multiple reading events);
   (v)   authors given sustained attention (authors with multiple reading events);
   (vi) actions caused by reading event (borrowing, sending, buying, transcrib-
         ing, attributions etc.);
   (vii) publications by language.

Each analysis offers a summary table and further interpretative discussion. Key
conclusions are analysed further in subsequent sections. As Table 1 suggests,
reading materials remain a central topic for the correspondence in each of the
seasons discussed here.

The evidence in the WLRD suggests that Birch and Yorke were great readers,
very interested in discussing their reading, their encounters with print and
manuscript of all kinds, and their knowledge of gossip in the book trade. The

---

[40] The WLRD is available at [URL to be determined: include link in text in electronic edition].

Table 1 Weekly Letter Reading Database: dimensions of the case study reading sample 1750–1754

Year	Weekly Letter date range	Birch letters	Yorke letters	Total letters	Enclosures	Reading events	Reading events per letter
1750	19 May to 17 Nov.	24	12	36	1	242	6.7
1751	29 June to Oct. 12	12	5	17	2	75	4.4
1752	23 May to 29 Nov.	21	10	31	1	162	5.2
1753	12 June to 3 Nov.	21	10	31	1	185	6.0
1754	6 July to 2 Nov.	15	9	24	2	178	7.4
Total		93	46	139	6	842	6.1

Weekly Letter adopted the self-deprecating irony and gentlemanly rhetoric of polite friendship associated with the republic of letters (see Figures 10 and 11). After the epistolary pleasantries that open the *commerce de lettres*, Birch, and also Yorke to a lesser extent, use the letter to record acts of reading, developing extended descriptions and debates on some books, periodicals and manuscripts. In addition, the letter also had an important function as a newsletter about books and manuscripts: which is to say, it provides news about books and manuscripts.

Analysis of the reading events for type and topic in Table 2 show that Birch and Yorke's interests were focussed on historical topics: history writing,

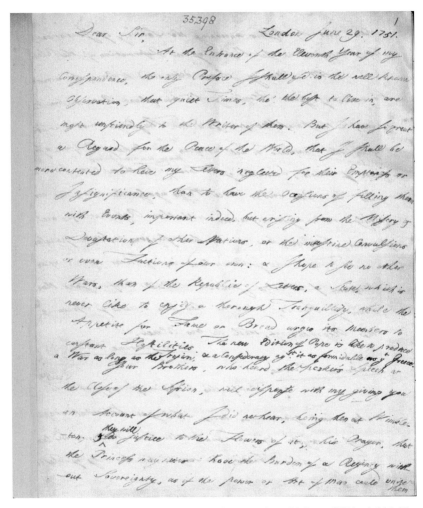

Figure 10 Thomas Birch to Philip Yorke, London, 29 June 1751, Add MS 35398, f. 1r. © The British Library Board

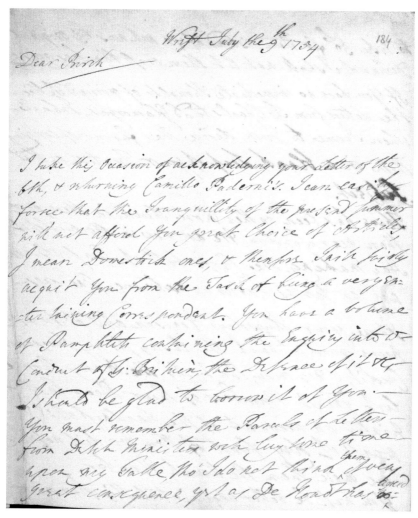

Figure 11 Yorke letter Yorke to Birch, Wrest July 9 1754, Add MS 35398,
f.184r. © The British Library Board

historical manuscripts and biography constituted 31 per cent of the discussion.
They had deep interests in tracts and pamphlets on religious debate and divinity
(8 per cent), and in literature (novels, poetry, plays, classics, theatre and satire
together making around 12 per cent of items discussed). Newspapers, news
reports (pamphlets and newsbooks) and economics took up 18 per cent of the
topics of discussion, with political pamphlets comprising a further 5 per cent.
Publications related to natural philosophy, including Royal Society papers,
science and medicine treatises, lectures and learned journals, variously in
print and manuscript, made up 16 per cent of the total.

Table 2 Weekly Letter Reading Database: type or kind of item in reading event

	Reading Events	%	Subject	Reading Events	%
Belles Lettres	524	62%			
			History	126	15
			Historical manuscripts	104	12
			Divinity	70	8
			Biography	37	4
			Poetry	34	4
			Philosophy	29	3
			Periodicals	24	3
			Criticism	15	2
			Novel	15	2
			Plays and Theatre	15	2
			Satire	15	2
			Travel	14	2
			Antiquities	13	2
			Letters	7	1
			Classics	6	1
Politics	154	18%			
			Newspaper	66	8
			News report	41	5
			Politics/satire	41	5
			Economics	6	1
Natural Philosophy	136	16%			
			Royal Society Paper	56	7
			Learned journal	29	3
			Scientific treatises	24	3
			Catalogue and Reference	12	1
			Medicine	8	1
			Lectures	7	1
Miscellaneous	30	4%			
			Publishing	8	1
			Maps	6	1
			Miscellaneous	16	2
	844	102%		844	102

Table 3 Weekly Letter Reading Database Format of reading-event items

Format	Reading Events	Percent %
Printed books and pamphlets	431	51
Manuscripts and manuscript collections	184	22
Newspapers	79	9
Periodicals and learned journals	59	7
Royal Society papers	57	7
Lectures	7	1
Others, including maps, prints, bookselling news, act of Parliament, broadsheets, prologues, proposals and regulations	27	3
	844	100

In terms of format (Table 3), Birch and Yorke primarily interacted with printed books and pamphlets (51 per cent), manuscripts (22 per cent) and newspapers and periodicals (16 per cent), but also papers and lectures delivered at the Royal Society and other learned institutions. The different formats, from comparatively long printed books or very substantial manuscript collections, to newspaper reports and periodical essays, and reading aloud or listening, are distinctly different kinds of reading events, as will be analysed later.

Although a key function of the Weekly Letter was, like a scribal newsletter, to give information about new publications and research discoveries, some publications and manuscripts were debated and discussed in more depth over repeated instances. Analysis of the data (Table 4) shows that 114 items have repeated mentions, comprising 409 data points (48 per cent of the total), while 435 items are unique reading events, almost always items that Birch notes without response from Yorke. (As this implies, the data consists of 549 discrete items). One conclusion here is that in general the Weekly Letter more often functioned as a newsletter indicating the literary landscape rather than being itself a space for extended deep debate and discussion. The next table explores those texts (books, periodicals and manuscripts) which garnered the most attention, with numerous mentions and extensive discussion. The 14 items that generate the greatest number of reading events are listed in Table 4.

This is a characteristic variety for the Weekly Letter, freely mixing manuscript material with printed books, newspapers and learned journals, with a notable focus on early modern history, Anglo-French relations and theology. The three most-discussed items include the two key research projects Birch

Table 4 Weekly Letter Reading Database sustained reading: reading events with multiple instances in different letters

Rank	Item title or name	Reading Events
1	Anthony Bacon Manuscripts, Lambeth, Bacon Papers, MS 647–62, 16 vols.	23
3=	Birch, Thomas, *Memoirs of the reign of Queen Elizabeth, from the year 1581 till her death* (London, 1754)	16
3=	Birch, Thomas, *The life of the most reverend Dr. John Tillotson, Lord Archbishop of Canterbury* (London, 1752)	16
4	*The London Evening-Post* (London, [1727–1806])	13
5	*The Evening Advertiser* (London, 1754–8)	10
6	Middleton, Conyers, *A vindication of the free inquiry into the miraculous powers, which are supposed to have subsisted in the Christian church* (London, 1751)	8
8=	Carte, Thomas, *A general history of England* (London, 1747–55)	7
8=	Forbes, Patrick, 'Transcripts of state letters and papers 1564–1587', BL: Add MS 4126	7
8=	Tucker, Josiah, *A letter to a friend concerning naturalizations: shewing, I. What a naturalization is not; II. What it is* (London, 1753)	7
11=	*Bibliothèque raisonnée des ouvrages des savans de l'Europe* (Amsterdam, 1728–53)	6
11=	Hyde, Henry, 2nd Earl of Clarendon: diary for the year 1688, BL: Stowe 770	6
11=	Jortin, John, *Remarks on ecclesiastical history* (London, 1751)	6
11=	*Journal Britannique*, ed. by Matthew Maty (La Haye, 1750–7)	6
11=	Lévesque, Prosper, *Mémoires pour servir à l'Histoire du Cardinal de Granvelle*. 2 vols. (Paris, 1753)	6

undertook in the period covered in this survey: the Bacon manuscripts from Lambeth Palace serve as the raw material for his history of Queen Elizabeth, amongst which the Forbes papers were also significant, as was Prosper

Lévesque's biography of Cardinal Antoine Perrenot de Granvelle (1517–86). Also in evidence is his use of printed newspapers and learned journals; and items related to particular literary and historical debates or political disputes. Conyers Middleton's posthumously published ninety-nine-page theological tract on miracles was a defence of his controversial *Free Inquiry* published in 1749, which was sceptical about miracles after the apostolic age, and as such, an attack on Catholic superstition. Protestant orthodoxy was also defended by John Jortin (1698–1770), an Anglican divine of Huguenot descent whose *Remarks* (1751) were an important statement of ecclesiastical history. Tucker's twenty-nine-page pamphlet on naturalisation, which Yorke had encouraged, was a contribution to the Jewish naturalisation debate of 1753, a cause promoted by Lord Hardwicke. Jortin and Maty were personal friends of Birch; Middleton was well known to the Yorkes' Cambridge circles and Tucker was a client of Yorke's. In addition to the individual texts that were accorded sustained attention, some authors were discussed repeatedly across many letters, for a variety of different writings, publications and texts.

Three groups of authors were discussed repeatedly, as indicated by Table 5. The first group comprises the historical figures that were the focus of Birch and Yorke's research: Anthony Bacon, Francis Bacon, Edward Lord Clarendon. The most frequently referenced author is Birch himself, although this is not as egocentric as it appears, as Birch no doubt felt obliged to account for his own literary activities to his primary patron, and the great majority of these reading events concern the progress of the publications he was working on in this period. The second group focusses on texts of the participants in intellectual controversies in the period from 1750 to 1754: Voltaire, Bolingbroke, Middleton, Warburton and Hoadly demonstrate the philosophical and theological seriousness of the Hardwicke Circle, their attraction to intellectual controversy, especially that promoted by those with whom they disagreed. For example, the Tory political philosopher Henry St John, viscount Bolingbroke, who had died in 1751, was the focus of much discussion about his intellectual legacy, most of it hostile, especially after David Mallet published his *Memoirs* in 1752 and his *Works* and *Philosophical Works* in 1754. The Deist Cambridge philosopher Conyers Middleton (1683–1750) died on 28 July 1750 while preparing two controversialist pamphlets for the press: these circumstances, the resulting pamphlet war and his legacy kept his works in discussion.[41]

The third group includes novelists (Richardson, Smollett), poets (Mallet, Whitehead) and historians (Carte, Forbes), whose work they followed,

---

[41] Middleton, *Examination of the bishop of London's discourses* (1750); *A vindication of the free inquiry* (1751).

Table 5 Weekly Letter Reading Database sustained reading: authors with multiple reading events

Author name	ODNB summary characterisation	Reading events
Birch, Thomas (1705–66)	compiler of histories and biographer	44
Bacon, Anthony (1558–1601)	spy	23
Voltaire, François-Marie Arouet [*known as* Voltaire] (1694–1778)	writer and philosopher	23
Middleton, Conyers (1683–1750)	Church of England clergyman and author	12
Tucker, Josiah (1713–99)	economist and political writer	11
Hill, Sir John (*bap.* 1714, *d.* 1775)	physician and actor	10
Warburton, William (1698–1779)	bishop of Gloucester and religious controversialist	10
Bolingbroke, Henry St John, styled first viscount Bolingbroke (1678–1751)	politician, diplomatist and author	9
Jortin, John (1698–1770)	ecclesiastical historian and literary critic	8
Carte, Thomas (*bap.* 1686, *d.* 1754)	historian	7
Forbes, Patrick (*d.* 1743)	[not in *ODNB*] historian	7
Johnson, Samuel (1709–84)	author and lexicographer	7
Richardson, Samuel (*bap.* 1689, *d.* 1761)	printer and author	7
Whitehead, William (*bap.* 1715, *d.* 1785)	poet and playwright	7
Stukeley, William (1687–1765)	antiquary and natural philosopher	7
Hyde, Edward, first earl of Clarendon (1609–74)	politician and historian	6
Bacon, Francis, Viscount St Alban (1561–1626)	lord chancellor, politician and philosopher	6
Lévesque, Prosper	[not in *ODNB*] French historian	6
Barre, Joseph (1692–1764)	[not in *ODNB*] French historian	5
Hoadly, Benjamin (1676–1761)	bishop of Winchester	5

Table 5 (cont.)

Author name	ODNB summary characterisation	Reading events
Mallet, David (1701/2?–65)	poet	5
Boyle, John, fifth earl of Cork and fifth earl of Orrery (1707–62)	biographer	5
Postlethwayt, Malachy (1707–67)	writer on economics and publicist	5
Smollett, Tobias George (1721–71)	writer	5

sometimes, as with the Jacobite Carte, with hostility. The satires of John Hill, discussed in Section 4, were a perennial fascination. Few of their notable authors were not writing in English (Voltaire, discussed in Section 4, Lévesque and Barre are the exceptions). Some of the figures were protegés of the Hardwickes, such as Tucker and Postlethwayt, both writers on political economy who had been formally encouraged by Birch and Yorke. Josiah Tucker was a Bristol-based clergyman whose writings on political economy and the Jewish naturalisation debate of 1753 appealed to Yorke's curiosity and the Hardwicke interest. The Rev. William Warburton (1698–1777) was a friend of Birch but his works of criticism, and his close association with, and edition, of Pope, attracted the ire of Philip and Charles Yorke. Warburton's publication of his reply to Bolingbroke, *A View of Lord Bolingbroke's Philosophy*, published in four parts in 1754–5, added to the discussion of both. Thomas Carte (1686–1754) was the subject of Birch and Yorke's antagonism as the author of a four-volume *History of England* (1747–55) that was the most significant Jacobite history of the period. It is notable that none of these authors are predominantly known as natural philosophers or men of science – although the French entomologist René Antoine Ferchault de Réaumur (1683–1757) achieved four reading events focussed on his work on bees and incubation. Further discussion of scientific topics will be found in Section 5; case studies of Birch's history writing, Bolingbroke and Warburton, Voltaire, and the novelists Hill, Richardson and Smollett appear in Section 4.

What these texts and authors have in common is the light they shine on Birch and Yorke's orthodox or loyal Hanoverian Whiggism: their reading leaned towards the historical figures of that tradition (especially English statesmen of the Protestant and parliamentary tradition) and modern protagonists of the administrative state while also vilifying Jacobites. Their habitual Francophobe Antigallicism was arguably more complex in natural philosophy, where they felt keenly the international rivalry between the Royal Society and the French

Table 6 Weekly Letter Reading Database: publications by language

Language	Reading Events	Percent
English	664	79
French	141	17
Latin	14	2
Untraced or unclear	7	1
Image	6	1
Map	5	1
Italian	4	>1
Dutch	3	>1
	844	101

Académie Royale des Sciences, but also valued the prestige associated with gift exchanges within the republic of letters, much of which was conducted in French (see Table 6). Birch and Yorke read very little in Latin, which was almost wholly the preserve of texts in the medical sciences.

3 Acts of Reading

What do Birch and Yorke do with the texts they encounter? What do the texts do to Birch and Yorke? In a variety of ways, these books and pamphlets provoke them to undertake further tasks and activities, to differing degrees, using diverse practices according to the text and the reader. The predominant activity Birch and Yorke did to texts was, simply, to notice them: identifying them by title and giving an indication to the other correspondent that such a book, pamphlet, poem, map, newspaper or manuscript had come to their attention, either in itself or by report, perhaps alongside further meta-level information about its production, sale, review or appearance. Noting books, in this sense, is the most common reading activity undertaken by Birch and Yorke, accounting for approximately half the events in the Weekly Letter. Even this apparently simple activity of 'noting and noticing' texts embeds a variety of activities, from simply listing titles to more substantial summarisation processes. In addition, Birch and Yorke note texts in order to do other actions with them, such as requests and commissions (location, purchase, dispatch, consignation); notes on progress through or preparation for the press; and actions of criticism such as attributions of anonymous publications. Case studies of these categories will be discussed in this section: as will be obvious, the identification of such activities is a complex disciplinary judgement as examples are often polyvalent, overlapping and fluid.

3.1 Noticing

Some reading events recorded in the Weekly Letter are uncomplicated. In September 1753, for example, Birch noted that 'Mr Wood's Account & Views of the Ruins of Palmyra are finish'd & ready for the Subscribers.' He added, 'I have seen a Copy complete.'[42] That was the only mention of this book: Yorke, it seems was not interested enough to note it in his response. But many reading events are more complex, inaugurating a series of critical observations. Birch, and less usually Yorke, made a habit of noting when he had come across a book or manuscript in his weekly travels, either firsthand or by report, whether it be new or old. Sometimes this was just to note a date when it was published (in October 1754, for example, Birch noted that the anonymous 'View of Lord Bolingbroke's Philosophy in four Letters to a Friend' had 'appear'd on Tuesday last', suggesting that it 'shews the hand of Dr. Warburton in every page').[43] Sometimes his encounters were more accidental: Birch described how, in June 1752, 'One of my suburb Rambles has lately thrown into my Way upon a Bulk in the Purlieus of Rag-fair a Rum,' a bookseller's term for an odd or unsaleable book. Rag Fair, in Houndsditch, was a secondhand clothing market. The book was 'a poem of the Rival of Dryden on the Stage, Elkanah Settle, tho' at the time of writing of it is reduc'd to the humbler condition of a Pensioner of the Charter House. It is intitled, Augusta Lacrimans: a Funeral poem on the Memory of the Honble Sr Daniel Wray Knt, printed in 1719 in fol'.[44] Settle (1648–1724) was one of the dunces of Pope's *Dunciad* in the 1727 edition. Birch, quoting eight lines of Settle's verse, enjoys the ironic juxtaposition of the bathetic panegyric of this odd book and their close friend Daniel Wray, who had recently been staying with Yorke at Wrest.

Birch and Yorke were notably interested in the whole life-cycle of books, from conception and writing to the progress of the manuscript through the press, the moment of publishing and its subsequent reception. Birch, for example, reported on 14 July 1750 that, when he had dined with Dr Foster at Eltham, he had learned that Gilbert West, who was very disabled with gout, planned to write something on the four Gospels.[45] No such volume appeared before West's death in 1756, although a few months after first discussing West's plans, Birch announced in November 1750 that ' Mr Gilbert West will I hope soon give us

---

[42] BL: Add MS 35398: Birch to Yorke, 29 September 1753, ff. 165–7 (167r).

[43] BL: Add MS 35398: Birch to Yorke, 5 October 1754, ff. 220–1 (221r); Warburton, *Lord Bolingbroke's philosophy*.

[44] BL: Add MS 35398: Birch to Yorke, 27 June 1752, ff. 60–1 (61r–v); Settle, *Augusta lacrimans* (1719). The only extant copy is in the British Library, presumably the one found by Birch, at BL: 11630.f.69.

[45] BL: Add MS 35397: Birch to Yorke, 14 July 1750, ff. 261–2.

another Canto of Spencer, which is thought by his Friends much superior to his former. It is upon <u>Education,</u> & of little favourable to that Plan of it, pursued in our Universities, that Oxford will perhaps regret the Honour they did him by his Degree of Doctor.'[46] West's Spencerian imitation *Education, a poem* appeared early the next year. Both Birch and Yorke prided themselves on staying ahead of the curve in literary news. They regularly announced to each other literary gossip about works in preparation: they describe sixty-two texts as 'in preparation'. New books and publishing news were a central currency in their exchange.

While at his country house, Yorke was hungry for whatever book news Birch in London could glean from the bookselling trade. In June 1752, Birch reported to Yorke that he had purchased some seventeenth-century volumes of French history from Baker the bookseller, who was selling a collection of books from the Jacobite historian Thomas Carte, who 'had resolv'd to quit this ungrateful town, & retire into Berkshire'.[47] On another occasion, Yorke asked Birch to go to the bookseller Paul Vaillant's shop on the Strand to buy a book for him – Marigni's *History of the Caliphs* – and have it sent to his London townhouse for direction onward to Scarborough, where he was travelling.[48] Foreign books were a curiosity for both Birch and Yorke. In 1752, for example, Birch noted that Vaillant had received a new shipment of French books, including 'a very disproportionate Number of Romances, a Species of writing, in which, since Marivaux's obstinate silence, France has been not at all eminent'.[49] The following year, Birch informed Yorke that Thomas Butler, a bookseller in Pall Mall, had 'imported a considerable Number of Books from Italy'.[50]

3.2 Attribution and Correction

Birch was tempted on seventeen occasions to supply authorial attributions for anonymous and pseudonymous works, though he was often incorrect. On 27 September 1750, for example, he wrote to Yorke about the recently published 'Occasional Prologue' spoken by Garrick at the opening of Drury Lane Theatre on 8 September 1750, the season when both theatres opened with the same play, *Romeo and Juliet*, and went head to head for twelve nights.[51] Birch

---

[46] BL: Add MS 35397: Birch to Yorke, 17 November 1750, ff. 320–1 (321r).
[47] BL: Add MS 35398: Birch to Yorke, 13 June 1752, ff. 56–7.
[48] BL: Add MS 35398: Yorke to Birch, Stocken [Hall, Lincolnshire], 24 June 1752, ff. 58–9; Marigny, *Histoire des califes* (1750).
[49] BL: Add MS 35398: Birch to Yorke, 14 October 1752, ff. 104–5.
[50] BL: Add MS 35398: Birch to Yorke, 25 August 1753, ff. 151–2.
[51] The 'Occasional Prologue' was published, for example, in *Whitehall Evening Post or London Intelligencer*, 22 September 1750.

commented, 'I conjecture by some peculiarity of style that the <u>Occasional Prologue</u> is Johnson's,' although in fact it later turned out to be by Garrick.[52] In August 1750, Birch noted a satire on Warburton's new critical edition of Alexander Pope's works, published with extensive commentary and notes in 1749.[53] The satire, called *A New Book of the Dunciad: occasion'd by Mr. Warburton's new Edition of the Dunciad Complete*, was attributed on its titlepage only to 'J. Scriblerus'. Birch and Yorke, though ideologically natural allies of Warburton, had in the past been irked by his ambition and self-regard, with the result they much enjoyed satires on his supposed pedantry. Of the *New Book of the Dunciad*, Birch reported it was

> an Attack upon Mr Warburton, & seems to be the production of Dr Hill, that universal Genius, who appears in some new shape or other. My reasons for ascribing it to him are very weighty ones because he is complimented both in the Text & Notes; & because I know few other Writers, who would condescend to satirize your old Client Mr Tho. Cooke of South Lambeth.[54]

Reading and acts of interpretation go together. Birch suggested that the *New Book of the Dunciad* was the work of the versatile satirist John Hill, whose target at this time was repeatedly the Royal Society.[55] Birch's supposition turned out not to be true: it was by the Rev. William Dodd.[56] In Dodd's poem, Warburton replaced Colley Cibber as King of the Dunces, using Warburton's new notes to Pope's poem as evidence of his intellectual failings. Birch reported that Wray was 'mortified that such Writers [as Hill] have declar'd ... against Warburton'.[57] In this example then, a simple act of reading enters the letter as a 'notice' of the pamphlet poem's publication, but is accompanied by a ramifying series of consequences, both critical (evaluation, (mis)attribution) and sociable (embarrassment, entertainment).

In 1752, Birch again argued that the recently published *Memoirs of the life and ministerial conduct ... of the late Lord Visc. Bolingbroke* (1752) 'are now thought to be the manufacture of Dr Hill, tho' they were at first ascrib'd to Mr Mallet. But the Falsities & Defects are too many & too gross to come from any Friend of his Ldps'.[58] Mallet was later shown to be the author. Birch was right, however, to attribute to Hill a role in *A Supplement to Mr. Chambers's Cyclopædia* (1753): it has, Birch said, 'too much of the hasty Compilation of Dr Hill in it to be any very valuable acquisition to the Public; & it is vastly overloaded with the least

---

[52] BL: Add MS 35397: Yorke to Birch, Wimple, 27 September 1750, ff. 295–7. The prologue was acknowledged in Garrick's *Poetical works* (1785), p. 102.

[53] Warburton's editions included Pope, *Essay on criticism* (1749) and *The Dunciad* (1749).

[54] BL: Add MS 35397: Birch to Yorke, 4 August 1750, ff. 269–70 (270r–v).

[55] Brant and Rousseau, *John Hill* (2017).   [56] Dodd, *A new book of the Dunciad* (1750).

[57] BL: Add MS 35397: Birch to Yorke, 4 August 1750, ff. 269–70 (270r–v).

[58] BL: Add MS 35398: Birch to Yorke, 11 November 1752, ff. 108–9.

interesting parts of Natural History, & particularly with Botany'.[59] Birch was incorrect in his attribution of two works that appeared in 1750 to Eliza Heywood: 'Mrs Eliza Heywood, who is a much more harmless Writer than the other two, notwithstanding her Novels & Romances of no very edifying a Tendency, is still living here, in spite of Brandy & viler Liquors, & instructing us weekly in her Tatler & Xtian Philosopher.'[60]

Birch valued his connections with printers and booksellers, and relayed news to Yorke of the progress of books through the press. Birch's descriptions of the business of book manufacture allowed Yorke an insider's view of the print shop and the machinery of learning. Birch was in demand as a proof corrector of scholarly publications, especially for the polite elite. In September 1750, Birch announced that 'Lord Orrery has actually put his Translation of Pliny to the press' of James Bettenham, 'with some corrections of the former Impression; I have already revis'd two of the Sheets from the press'.[61] To act as the final proof corrector for Orrery was for Birch a position of some prestige. In 1753, he commented on the correcting process of Isaac Hawkins Browne's neo-Latin poem 'On the Immortality of the Soul'.[62] He described how Browne had delayed the publication, which had 'been in the Press for five months' through his own folly, keeping a proof sheet in his pocket for several weeks without making corrections.[63]

3.3 Requesting and Sending

Lending and sending books between Birch and Yorke constituted an important collaborative activity within their circle. Yorke repeated requests to Birch to be sent books and manuscripts related to his historical research, the world of learning and political news. Birch was often called on to locate the book and pass it on to subalterns for transmission. The larger volumes Yorke requested were not sent by post like a letter, but required a human mediator, a servant, carrier or cart. The 'Porter' at St James's Square was an important intermediary for sending items from the house. The Yorkes also maintained a weekly carrier throughout the summer months between London and Wrest, as did Lord Hardwicke between his house in London and his country estate Wimpole near Cambridge.

---

[59] BL: Add MS 35398: Birch to Yorke, 27 October 1753, ff. 175–6.

[60] BL: Add MS 35397: Birch to Yorke, 15 September 1750, ff. 289–92. *The tatler revived* (1750); *The Christian philosopher* (1750–1). Patrick Spedding (in *A bibliography of Eliza Haywood*, pp. 660–1) rejects the attribution to Haywood on compelling stylistic grounds.

[61] BL: Add MS 35397: Birch to Yorke, 15 September 1750, ff. 289–92 (291r). Boyle, earl of Orrery, *Letters of Pliny* (1751).

[62] Browne, *De animi immortalitate. Poema*.

[63] BL: Add MS 35398: Birch to Yorke, 28 July 1753, ff.138r–140r (138v).

Some of the books Yorke requested were recent publications he had read about in newspapers. In July 1750, for example, Lady Grey wrote to Birch asking him to send Wrest the recently published second volume of Carte's *History of England*, ready for Yorke's return from Wimpole.[64] In October, when Yorke asked Birch to make a holiday visit to Wrest, he asked him to bring two recently published popular prose fictions with him: 'the Acct of Maclain in your Pocket, & Jo Thompsons Adventures if they are not bad'.[65] The first was a criminal biography of 'Captain' James Maclean (or Maclaine), the 'gentleman highwayman' executed at Tyburn on 3 October.[66] The account of Maclean's life, Birch later said, was undertaken by 'Dr Allen, an honest Dissenting Minister, & Doctor of Physic', and 'his Account of that unhappy man is a sensible & pathetic piece'.[67] The second item was Edward Kimber's (1719–69) *The Life and Adventures of Joe Thompson*, a two-volume picaresque ramble novel in the manner of Defoe. Birch refused the invitation to visit, but must have sent the books anyway, for when Yorke planned his return to London in November, Birch asked him, in a horizontal postscript to the letter: 'You will not forget to bring with you Mr Toll's Reply to Church, & Dr Allen's Account of Maclaine.'[68] So although Birch valued the criminal biography and the Rev. Frederick Toll's pamphlet on miracles, it seems he could do without Kimber's novel.

Other requests were for older and rarer books. In July and August 1750, Yorke asked Birch to send him 'Strype's Life of S J Cheke & that of cardinal Amboise', the first published in 1705 and the second in 1631, together with another book that Yorke's brother John was going to describe in person when he saw him.[69] Yorke further asked Birch to call at the shop of W. Meyer, a bookseller in in May's Buildings near St Martin's Lane who specialised in French books, '& tell him, I wonder he has not sent me for some time any *Journaux des Savans*', a French learned journal.[70] A few days later, Birch replied:

> I have not yet had the pleasure of seeing your Brother John since his return to Town, & therefore can say nothing to the Book about which your Letter refers

---

[64] BL: Add MS 35397: Jemima Lady Grey to Birch, Wrest, 12 July 1750, ff. 259–60; Carte, *General history of England*, vol. II (1750).

[65] BL: Add MS 35397: Yorke to Birch, Wrest, 11 October 1750, ff. 302–3 (303r).

[66] *Compleat history of James Maclean* (1750).

[67] BL: Add MS 35397: Birch to Yorke, 13 October 1750, ff. 304–5 (304v).

[68] BL: Add MS 35397: Birch to Yorke, 17 November 1750, ff. 320–1, p. 321r; Toll, *Some remarks* (1750).

[69] BL: Add MS 35397: Yorke to Birch, Wrest, 31 July 1750, ff. 267–8 (268r); Strype, *Life of John Cheke* (1705); *La vie du Cardinal D'Amboise* (1631).

[70] *Le journal des Sçavans* (Amsterdam, 1665–1792).

me to him. Cardinal D'Amboise's Life is in my Study, but that of St John
Cheke is neither there nor in any of the Booksellers Shops, where I have
inquir'd for it. It is indeed much the scarcest of Mr. Strype's Works; but you
have an ample Abridgement of it in the General Dictionary.[71]

Birch was eventually able to find a copy of Strype on Cheke in the 'unlending
shelves' of their mutual friend Daniel Wray, who, Birch said, 'perhaps the more
readily parted with it from the Contempt which he has for that Performance'.
Birch sent it to Wrest along with 'The Life of Cardinal D'Amboise & Des
Maizeaux's Collection of Ana'.[72] As Birch's exertions suggest, these requests
for books and manuscripts are often quite onerous and time-consuming, reinfor-
cing the human network forged around Yorke and Birch, and the Hardwicke
Circle more generally. Such labours underlined the intimate quality of their
exchanges: Birch sometimes sent his personal copy or went to Yorke's own
library in his St James' Square townhouse to find one. Even though Birch,
acting at Yorke's behest, has the subaltern position, their correspondence is
marked by the language of trust and friendship, patronage and servility.

Manuscripts were also discussed when found, seen or identified. The letters
of October and November 1750 buzzed with excitement about Birch's discoveries. In this period, Birch was reading and transcribing the correspondence of
the Elizabethan spy Anthony Bacon (1558–1601). In August, Yorke had
acquired, possibly from the bookseller Thomas Osborne, four volumes of
manuscript letters by Christophe de Harlay, Comte de Beaumont, the French
ambassador in England from 1602 to 1605.[73] He was somewhat disappointed
with his purchase: 'I think [him] no great man, but imperfectly informed of our
Matters & tedious in his own Reflections.'[74] In October, he heard about the
discovery of the papers of Sir Edward Nicholas at West-Horsley Place, the
country house of Henry Pelham Clinton, second duke of Newcastle. Nicholas
was a royalist administrator who had been Secretary of State for Charles I and
then for Charles II after the Restoration.[75] Yorke had been pressing Birch to visit
the 'Nicholasian Archive', as he called it, since 1748.[76] On 27 October, Birch
related that his friend Sir John Evelyn (1682–1763)' has brought away from
West-Horsley a large Cloke-bag full of Secretary Nicholas's Papers, besides six

---

[71] BL: Add MS 35397: Birch to Yorke, 4 August 1750, ff. 269–70 (269r).
[72] BL: Add MS 35397: Birch to Yorke, 11 August 1750, ff. 274–5 (274); Des Maizeaux,
   Scaligerana, (1740).
[73] BL: Add MS 35397: Yorke to Birch, Wrest, 16 August 1750, ff. 271–2; Birch published
   translations of Beaumont's court letters in *Memoirs of the reign of Queen Elizabeth* (1754).
[74] BL: Add MS 35397: Yorke to Birch, Wrest, 1 November 1750, ff. 312–13.
[75] Nicholas, *Mr Secretary Nicholas* (1955); Nicholas, *Nicholas papers* (1886–1920).
[76] BL: Add MS 35397: Yorke to Birch, 28 June 1748, ff. 123–4; Yorke to Birch, Wrest, 7 July 1748,
   ff. 129–30.

Volumes of Copies of his Letters. He removes with his family immediately to Town for the Winter, & will bring up the whole Collection with him, which he says he shall most readily gratify you & me with the Perusal of'.[77] Yorke replied, 'I shall be much obliged to Sir John Evelyn for a sight of old Scy Nicholas's Papers, & shall be ready for them when I come to Town,'[78] repeating his readiness for 'any bundles of the Old Secy (which are not of his own hand, or rather Scrawl)' a few weeks later.[79] Birch made transcripts of some of the Nicholas Papers between 18 December 1750 and 1 February 1751, the originals of which are now lost.[80] Such was Yorke's impatience for new material that some of the transcripts were sent to Wrest.

Some manuscripts were more elusive than others. In June 1753, James Yorke wrote to Birch on behalf of Yorke, asking him to send the third volume of Sir Thomas Roe's papers to Wrest, which had been misplaced.[81] Roe (1581?–1644) was an English diplomat who attended the peace conferences at Regensburg and Vienna in 1638–42, at the conclusion of the Thirty Years' War. Birch had borrowed Roe's letter-books, amounting to five volumes, from Samuel Richardson, who had published the first volume for the Society for the Encouragement of Learning in 1740.[82] James Yorke asked Birch to search for the third volume again – 're-examine your Study with the ye utmost attention' – and, if it was not found there, to enquire about it with Richardson. A few days later, Philip Yorke asked again for the third volume of Roe, if it could be found anywhere, and, if it was not deep in what he called Birch's 'Barathrum' (abyss or hell), Yorke suggested it might have been included in a 'Sack of Papers' returned to Richardson, noting that 'the last vol: of his Letters is amongst the Harleian Mss, & the late Ld Oxford wd have done but justice in restoring it to the Body of the Collection'.[83] Birch searched for the Roe volume again and related that, though it was not in his house, Richardson would search his when at leisure.[84] More than a year later, Birch announced he had found the missing volume in his study, 'under some other Books which conceal'd it from me'. He sent it to Wrest the same week, with four other volumes.[85]

---

[77] BL: Add MS 35397: Birch to Yorke, 27 October 1750, ff. 308–11 (308r–v). Evelyn had found the Nicholas papers at Horsley in 1750; BL: Add MS 35397: Birch to Yorke, 6 October 1750, ff. 300–1.

[78] BL: Add MS 35397: Yorke to Birch, Wrest, 1 November 1750, ff. 312–13 (312v–313r).

[79] BL: Add MS 35397: Yorke to Birch, Wrest, 15 November 1750, ff. 318–19 (318r).

[80] BL: Add MS 4180: Thomas Birch, 'Extracts of the State Papers and Letters of Sr Edward Nicholas from the originals lately in the possession of his grandson William Nicholas, Esq, and now in that of Sr John Evelyn, Bart'.

[81] BL: Add MS 35398: James Yorke to Birch, Wrest, 24 June 1753, ff. 122–3 (122r).

[82] Roe, *Negotiations* (1740). Birch's copy, with MS notes, is BL: Add MS 1854.h.6.

[83] BL: Add MS 35398: Yorke to Birch, Wrest, 28 June 1753, ff. 124–5 (124r).

[84] BL: Add MS 35398: Birch to Yorke, 30 June 1753, ff. 126–7 (126r).

[85] BL: Add MS 35398: Birch to Yorke, 17 August 1754, ff. 190–3 (193v).

3.4 Summarisation and Transcription

Some forms of reading were notably more laborious than others. For papers read at the Royal Society, Birch, as secretary, was expected to make a summary for the Journal Book, a practice he borrowed for many Weekly Letters too (see Section 5).[86] Transcription was an important method for acquiring historical information for retrieval and sharing, in the absence of mechanical methods for the reproduction of manuscripts. Birch undertook large-scale transcription projects himself, rarely if ever subcontracting or trusting the process to amanuenses. In July 1752, for example, the Weekly Letter records that Birch was transcribing extracts from the Earl of Clarendon's diary for 1688:

> It is the original Diary of Henry, the second Earl of Clarendon during the memorable Year 1688, containing 168 pages in folio. I am transcribing the chief passages in it, which will give you some entertainment, as they relate Conversations with King James & his Queen, princess Anne of Denmark, the prince of Orange, Lord Chancellor Jeffreys, &c. besides many Facts, to which our Historians are intire Strangers.[87]

Letters throughout August relate that Birch was busy transcribing the diary: at the end of the month, Yorke asks to read the transcripts (along with a prepublication copy of Birch's *Life of Tillotson* if the booksellers would release it).[88] Birch replies by sending the Tillotson to Wrest, but regrets the Clarendon transcript has already been borrowed by his father, Lord Hardwicke. Yorke finally got the diary transcript in September, when he was 'entertained' by it, though it was the 'Performance of an honest but weak man'.[89]

Yorke occasionally abused Birch's facility in manuscript transcription. In September 1754, Yorke asked Birch to transcribe a 'pretty singular' paper in the Harleian Library ('in one of the Volumes of Royal letters, wch are in the Closet'), of an 'Examination' signed by Bacon, Winwood & other Privy Councellors'. The state had acquired the Harleian Library in 1753 for £10,000 as the basis of the British Museum manuscripts collection; at this juncture it was still located in a single room with two closets at the bottom of the garden of the Countess of Orford's house in Dover Street.[90] 'As marks by wch you may know the Paper', Yorke related some of the odd things it records, such as a story about

---

[86] Royal Society: Journal Book Original, JBO/22, 1751–4.
[87] BL: Add MS 35398: Birch to Yorke, 25 July 1752, ff. 73–4 (74r). The original diary is BL: Stowe 770: Diary of Henry Hyde, second earl of Clarendon, for the year 1688.
[88] BL: Add MS 35398: Birch to Yorke, 1 August 1752, ff. 77–8; BL: Add MS 35852: Birch transcript: 'Extracts of the Diary of Henry Earl of Clarendon, beginning Jan. 1st, 1687/8, and ending 31 Dec. 1688'.
[89] BL: Add MS 35398: Yorke to Birch, Wimpole, 19 September 1752, ff. 91–2 (91v).
[90] Harris, *British Museum*, p. 3.

'enclosing a treasonable libel in an apple' and a reference to a Sicilian massacre, presumably the Sicilian Vespers of 1282 that began the revolt against Charles I, Angevin King of Sicily.[91] Three weeks later, Birch sent him a transcribed letter from the Harleian Library entitled 'Interrogatories, whereupon Peacham is to be examined, Harleian MSS 19 Jan 1614', which he believed most closely fitted the description.[92] However, as Birch notes ruefully, it does not mention either of the odd anecdotes, neither that of a libel in an apple nor of the Sicilian massacres, and, as Yorke was quick to note, it was not the correct one.[93] Three weeks later, Birch sent another transcript: a letter dated 22 January 1613 from 'Fr Bacon, H Montagu and H Yelverton', on 'Cotton's cause', 'touching the book, & the letter in the gilt apple', but no Sicilian massacre.[94] At the end of the month, Yorke thanked Birch for the letter from the Harleian Library: the transcript was indeed the one, but jumbled in his memory.[95] Yorke's willingness to absorb considerable quantities of Birch's time and effort for his own whim must have sorely tested Birch and testifies to the value of Yorke's patronage for Birch.

4 Reading Literature and History: Case Studies

Analysis of the reading-event data in Table 2 ('Type or Kind') shows that Birch and Yorke's interests were primarily focussed on historical topics: history writing and historical manuscripts constituted 27 per cent of the topics of discussion. But they also had deep interests in tracts and pamphlets on religious debate and divinity (8 per cent) and in literature (novels, poetry, plays, classics, theatre, biography or memoir, criticism, travel writing and satire together comprise approximately 28 per cent of the items discussed). The topic of history was prominent in part because of Birch's own activities as a writer of history and also as a literary editor. The Weekly Letter records how he undertook a series of specialist scholarly book-related activities such as transcription of historical manuscripts, writing and compilation of history and seeing the book through the press (including proof correction). Birch and Yorke's own contribution to history writing is focussed on publications of 'State Papers' that make a documentary record of sixteenth- and seventeenth-century British history and international relations. While their own history writing is strongly marked by

---

[91] BL: Add MS 35398: Yorke to Birch, Wrest, 5 September 1754, ff. 206–7.
[92] BL: Add MS 35398: Birch transcript: '"Interrogatories, whereupon Peacham us to be examined", Harleian Mss', enclosure: ff. 224–5.
[93] BL: Add MS 35398: Birch to Yorke, 28 September 1754, ff. 216–17.
[94] BL: Add MS 35398: Birch to Yorke, 19 October 1754, ff. 229–32.
[95] BL: Add MS 35398: Yorke to Birch, Wrest, 30 October 1754, ff. 240–1. The letter is printed in Bacon, *Works*, ed. Montagu, XII, pp 469–71.

orthodox Court-Whig politics, they also paid close attention to rival historical projects, especially by Jacobite historians such as Thomas Carte. This section explores some case studies in more detail: Birch's history writing; Birch and Yorke's engagement with philosophers (Bolingbroke, and Voltaire); and the novelists Richardson, Hill and Smollett. Section 5 considers their engagement with natural philosophy (16 per cent of reading events). These case studies allow a closer historical focus on the kinds of conversation about books and publications Birch and Yorke entertained.

4.1 Writing History: Birch, Bacon and Queen Elizabeth

The first case study focusses on the Weekly Letter's discussion of Birch's historical research and publications. The Weekly Letter traces in detail, for example, the progress of Birch's *Memoirs of the Reign of Queen Elizabeth, from the Year 1581 till her Death*, which was published in 1754 by Andrew Millar and dedicated to Yorke. This was primarily based on Birch's research in the historical papers of Anthony Bacon, sixteen volumes of which Birch had located in the Library at Lambeth Palace in August 1748.[96] Bacon was the nephew of the lord treasurer, William Cecil, Lord Burghley, and, with Robert Devereux, second earl of Essex, masterminded Queen Elizabeth's large-scale foreign intelligence operation in Europe in the 1590s. The Elizabethan period was a core interest for the Hardwicke's Whig conception of British history, for it was during this period, they reasoned, that a free and independent England had liberated itself from Catholic tyranny. Birch opened his history with the statement:

> The reign of queen Elizabeth is less distinguish'd by its length, than by the vigour and success of her government, . . . the establishment of the reforma-tion of religion, . . . the support of the protestant interest, [and] her triumph over the whole force of Spain more than once combin'd for her destruction: And the vast improvement of the naval strength and commerce of the nation.

Birch's historiographical interest was not to write another narrative history of Elizabeth's reign, but rather to give an account of the 'secret intrigues' of her favourite, Robert, earl of Essex, as revealed in the recently discovered private papers of his 'intimate friend' Anthony Bacon. 'To relate over again the same series of transactions diversified only in the method and style, and with the

---

[96] Lambeth: Bacon Papers, BL: Add MS 647–62, 16 vols. Birch received a letter of introduction from the archbishop in August 1748 (BL: Add MS 35397: Birch to Yorke, 18 August 1748, ff. 145–6) and in a visit in October found the sixteen-volume collection (BL: Add MS 35397: Birch to Yorke, 15 October 1748, ff. 176–7).

addition of a few particular incidents, would be no very agreeable undertaking to the historian, and certainly of little use to the reader.'[97] Instead, he turned to 'authentic memorials', carefully selected, so as 'to open the true springs' of 'political conduct' in Elizabeth's reign.

In 1750, Yorke reiterated his desire to learn more about the Bacon materials Birch had identified in the library at Lambeth Palace. In June, Birch announced that Archbishop Thomas Herring, a close friend of Lord Hardwicke, had allowed Birch to borrow the manuscript volumes from his library, volume by volume. 'He had the Goodness to promise me of his own Accord to dispense with the Rules establish'd with respect to the Lambeth Manuscripts, in my favour, & to allow me to the Use of Anthony Bacon's papers at my own House, upon my giving a Receipt to Mr. Hall, the Library Keeper.'[98]

A few weeks later, Birch noted that 'the ArchBp put into my hands the first Volume of Anth. Bacon's papers. It contains those to the year 1590 during his Travels till his return to England.'[99] Birch continued to work on these manuscripts through the summer, commenting every few weeks on the progress of his transcriptions, which he then sent to Wrest for Yorke to read.[100] After a year, he was up to the twelfth volume and was already writing *Memoirs*.[101] In June 1752, he wrote that the book had 'already swell'd to the Bulk of six & twenty Sheets in print out of Seventy or eighty, of which the whole is to consist'.[102] Yorke commented on Birch's project at length in his reply, in a revealing description of his expectations for the history.

> I am glad Antony Bacon goes on prosperously but I shall be a severe Critick over it; You have time enough before you, & I wd have it a complete Pattern of Compilation. I shall admit of no details of minute occurrences, no repetition of Events better related in common Histories, – no interruption of the Narration wth immaterial dates, – no loading of the Text wth a pedantic antiquated Jargon like Naunton's – in short a nothing but what shall pass the

---

[97] Birch, *Memoirs of Queen Elizabeth*, I, pp. 1, 2.
[98] BL: Add MS 35397: Birch to Yorke, 23 June 1750, ff. 249–52.
[99] BL: Add MS 35397: Birch to Yorke, 30 June 1750, ff. 253–4.
[100] For example, he noted that he 'return'd yesterday Morning the second Volume of Anthony Bacon's papers to the Archbp, & receiv'd from him the third' (BL: Add MS 35397: Birch to Yorke, 18 August 1750, ff. 276–7). 'My extracts of the first Volume amount to 373 pages in 4to those of the second to 170 pages; & I have already transcrib'd 94 pages of the third' (BL: Add MS 35397: Birch to Yorke, 1 September 1750, ff. 282–3 (283v)). Later in September, he sent his transcripts to Yorke at Wrest (BL: Add MS 35397: Birch to Yorke, 15 September 1750, ff. 289–92). Yorke commented that Birch had made 'very copious' transcripts of the Bacon material and might have been more sparing in those relating 'the Domestick Affairs of the family' (BL: Add MS 35397: Yorke to Birch, Wimple, 27 September 1750, ff. 295–6).
[101] BL: Add MS 35398: Birch to Yorke, 14 September 1751, ff. 31–2. Birch 'finish'd the XIV volume of Ant. Bacon' (BL: Add MS 35398: Birch to Yorke, 28 September 1751, ff. 37–8).
[102] BL: Add MS 35398: Birch to Yorke, 13 June 1752, ff. 56–7 (56r).

severest test, & unite the Truth & Marrow of History with the elegance & spirit of classical Composition. Your plan of drawing it out at length, in order to reduce & polish it afterwards, is a very good one, – & will give you an opportunity of consulting your Friends on doubtful places.[103]

The model to avoid, Yorke suggested, was Robert Naunton's *Fragmenta regalia* (1641). Naunton was a superannuated courtier who offered advice to Elizabeth I in the form of character sketches of her courtiers, written in ornate prose strewn with Latinate humanist terms. In preference, Yorke proposed Birch should pursue an extended orthodox narrative history, stressing the propriety of method and pattern. Advice and criticism of this kind was offered within the privacy of the coterie. Among themselves, they referred to their practices of criticism and advice as belonging to the 'Licenser's Bureau', with the position of the licenser usually ascribed to Daniel Wray. The name made a joking analogy to the system of censorship established in 1662 by the Licensing of the Press Act (14 Car. II. c. 33), which appointed Roger L'Estrange as licenser of the press, responsible for preventing the publication of seditious, irreligious, pernicious and scandalous books and pamphlets by only permitting those approved by the licenser to be published.[104] In the Hardwicke Circle, Wray's role as licenser seems more like a cross between advanced proof correcter and fact checker. The process was important to Yorke, however: in September 1752, he complained to Birch that 'Wray & you have never met upon the Introduction to A Bacon, surely the Licenser's Bureau shd be more respected.'[105]

A year later, on 23 June 1753, Birch advised Yorke that the book was complete and was to be sent to the printer next week, to make a book in two quarto volumes of about sixty sheets each (more than a thousand pages in total). There followed a long debate between the two about Birch's contract with Andrew Millar, the bookseller, about whom Wray had told a story 'wch shews him to be of the malignant cast'.[106] Birch had an offer of 100 guineas for the copy, which he had turned down, and instead had agreed to a deal wherein Millar was to pay for the paper and printing and receive a little for the risk, and Birch was to get all the profit.[107] Yorke complained, 'He shall reap the Fruits of your labours gratis,' and said he had 'once shadowed out your Work to Dodsley my Neighbour, in a way that made his mouth water, as I thought, & c[oul]d He have prevailed on Ld C – d [Chesterfield] to recommend

---

[103] BL: Add MS 35398: Yorke to Birch, Stocken, 24 June 1752, ff. 58–9 (59r).
[104] Nipps, 'Cum privilegio', pp. 494–500.
[105] BL: Add MS 35398: Yorke to Birch, Wimpole, 19 September 1752, ff. 91–2.
[106] BL: Add MS 35398: Yorke to Birch, Wimpole, 19 September 1752, ff. 91–2.
[107] BL: Add MS 35398: Birch to Yorke, 23 June 1753, ff. 120–1.

it in the <u>World</u>, no Novel of Fieldings or Lennox's (I am perswaded) wd have sold better'.

Robert Dodsley's shop at the sign of Tully's Head at No. 52 Pall Mall was in the 1750s the most fashionable place of assembly for the literati, from where Dodsley and Lord Chesterfield published the essay periodical *The World*. A week later, Birch explained the terms of his 'bargain' with Millar in even more detail, giving details of the costs of printing and binding the five hundred copies at £289; the sale of which would yield £450, sold at 18 shillings to the booksellers (and directly by Birch to gentlemen at a guinea). The profit of £161 was to be divided between the bookseller and author.[108] Yorke was still not satisfied: two weeks later, Birch spelled it out for Yorke. Millar was to get 10 per cent of the profits for his 'risque', which would net Birch £140 if all the copies were sold.[109] These terms, Birch explained, sufficiently lowered the risk to Millar to allow the venture to proceed. The book was eventually published on 10 January 1754.[110] In August 1754, Birch informed Yorke that a gift copy of the *Memoirs* was 'in the hands of the Book binder, & will, when finish'd be sent to St James's Square',[111] along with some other books and a copy of Birch's earlier *An Historical View of the Negotiations between the Courts of England, France, and Brussels, from the year 1592 to 1617*, published by Millar in 1749.[112]

The cumulative effect of the discussion of Birch's progress with the history is curious: Birch is patient but testy with some of Yorke's enquiries, especially about his publishing contract with Millar. But the overall tone is of discipline and surveillance. Birch is proud of his speed of composition and enjoys reporting on his progress to Yorke, who likes knowing about the book's progress, reads drafts and transcripts and offers his (and his family's) support and patronage. The book is facilitated by Yorke's influence. In return, Birch offers an insider view of the process of its research and composition. The book announces this patronage in its dedication (volume one to Yorke and volume two to his brother Charles Yorke). This is good lesson in Hardwicke Circle workings: the Weekly Letter is more like a surveillance mechanism than an 'actual venue of intellectual practice', as Larry Klein characterises the role of the salon in the republic of letters.[113] In its role as a newsletter, the Weekly Letter advertises texts and topics that are articulated and debated elsewhere,

---

[108] BL: Add MS 35398: Birch to Yorke, 30 June 1753, ff. 126–7.
[109] BL: Add MS 35398: Birch to Yorke, 14 July 1753, ff. 132–3.
[110] *Public advertiser*, 8 January 1754.
[111] BL: Add MS 35398: Birch to Yorke, 17 August 1754, ff. 190–3.
[112] This copy of Birch's *Historical View* is in the library at Hardwicke's house, National Trust Wimpole. BL: Add MS 35398: Birch to Yorke, 17 August 1754, ff. 190–3 (193r–v).
[113] Klein, 'Gender, conversation', p. 103.

whether in face-to-face conversations, sociable assemblies and institutional meetings or in the wider print culture. The Weekly Letter correspondence maintains the operation of the Hardwicke Circle, gathering intelligence that can be deployed for other purposes in the influence business.

4.2 Philosophers: Bolingbroke and Voltaire

Birch and Yorke were well informed about the wider currents of Enlightenment and European philosophy, although their interest in it was highly partisan. As Tables 4 and 5 show, amongst their most sustained reading were philosophically serious writers such as Voltaire, Bolingbroke, Warburton and Middleton, as well as a writer on commerce and economic theory, the Rev. Josiah Tucker of Bristol. They also took notice of, in a less sustained manner, other significant contributions to moral philosophy in the period, including Montesquieu's *De l'esprit des lois* (1748) and Francis Hutcheson's *A System of Moral Philosophy* (1755).[114] It is perhaps telling that their attention here was more often held by controversy and scandal than philosophical significance.

The legacy of Henry St John, Viscount Bolingbroke, occupied a considerable amount of attention in Birch's contributions to the Weekly Letter 1750–4. Bolingbroke was an influential Tory statesmen in the early eighteenth century, but, by 1750, aged seventy-two, he was in declining health and living in Battersea. As Court Whigs, the Hardwickes were naturally in opposition to his interest, although as Lord Chancellor, Lord Hardwicke continued a correspondence with him. Birch found much to criticise: he was hostile to Bolingbroke as a former Jacobite, a Tory, a Freethinker, a Deist and a historian. Birch kept Yorke informed about his condition through 1749 and 1750, noting that he was ill with a swelling in his cheek, perhaps a cancer, and had committed its cure to an 'illiterate Irish Pretender', a quack who offered 'a Nostrum for such Complaints'.[115] Following Bolingbroke's death in December 1751, Birch and Yorke assessed and debated his legacy and influence as it was brought into focus by new editions, posthumous publications and memoirs, responses and criticisms. Even his death excited controversy. Birch reported gossip from a clergyman friend that Bolingbroke did not attend divine services or take the sacraments in the last four years of his life. They were both outraged by the self-serving and perhaps autobiographical account of his life engraved on his grand memorial monument by Louis-Francois Roubiliac in St Mary's Battersea, which denied he was ever a Jacobite: he claimed his 'Persecution' was caused

---

[114] Montesquieu: BL: Add MS 35397: Yorke to Birch, Wrest, 1 November 1750, ff. 312–13 (312r); Hutcheson: BL: Add MS 35398: Birch to Yorke, 6 July 1754, ff. 182–3 (183v).

[115] BL: Add MS 35397: Birch to Yorke, 8 September 1750, 284–5; Add MS 35398: Birch to Yorke, 24 August 1751, ff. 16–17.

by his attachment to Queen Anne and he was 'The Enemy of no national Party; The Friend of no Faction'.[116]

Bolingbroke's literary executor was the Scottish poet and playwright David Mallet, who set about publishing Bolingbroke's works, notably including the controversial pieces previously circulated only in manuscript, private publications or suppressed piracies. Mallet began with *Letters on the Study and Use of History* in March 1752 (a date which falls outside the Weekly Letter season for that year). As a historian, Bolingbroke attracted a storm of anger at his suggestion that ancient history, both secular and sacred, was not firmly established by evidence and could not be accepted as history. The first publication noticed in the Weekly Letter, on 4 July 1752, was described as:

> A new philosophical piece of Lord Bolingbroke of 83 pages in 8° has appeared this Week under the title of <u>Reflections concerning innate Moral Principles,</u> translated from the French, in which language the translator says he wrote it for the use of a Noble Club at Paris, of which he was a Member, the original having been published there since his death.[117]

In Birch's summary, Bolingbroke's

> Design is to explode all innate principles of Morality; he denies even Compassion & Filial Affection to the Interests of Nature; the only principle, which he admits as born with Man, & inseparable from his Nature, being the Love of that, which gives him pleasure, & an Aversion to pain; Self Love being the governing principle in Mankind.[118]

Birch's summary does not express his disapproval explicitly, although its unvarnished view of Bolingbroke's materialism makes explicit that Bolingbroke's state of nature was not based on compassion and sociability, but was rather more like Hobbes's version of self-love.

Birch first noticed Mallet's plans for Bolingbroke's *Works* in September 1752, stating that it was to be a substantial venture with five volumes in quarto.[119] In November 1752, Birch also noted the publication of Mallet's *Memoirs of the late Lord Visc. Bolingbroke*, where Birch conjectured about who might be the author.[120] Mallet's edition of Bolingbroke did not appear until 1754, and then in a dual edition of his *Works* and his *Philosophical Works*, each in five volumes. When asked by Yorke to quiz the publisher Millar about them in October 1753, Birch reassured him that 'Lord Bolingbroke's Works will

---

[116] Bolingbroke Memorial, St Mary's Battersea, London.
[117] BL: Add MS 35398: Birch to Yorke, 4 July 1752, ff. 62–3 (63r–v).
[118] BL: Add MS 35398: Birch to Yorke, 4 July 1752, ff. 62–3 (63v); Bolingbroke, *Reflections concerning innate moral principles* (1752).
[119] BL: Add MS 35398: Birch to Yorke, 30 September 1752, ff. 97–9 (97v).
[120] BL: Add MS 35398: Birch to Yorke, 11 November 1752, ff. 108–9 (109v).

undoubtedly appear intire, as soon as the Season of Publication is a little more advanc'd.'[121] The *Works* finally appeared in March 1754, and the *Philosophical Works*, collecting the controversial unpublished and privately published pieces, followed in June 1754.

The scandal surrounding Bolingbroke's *Letters on History*, especially its attack on the evidence and authenticity of the Gospels, occupied much attention. A broad coalition of readers, from Anglican divines to Whig apologists, were outraged by Bolingbroke's attack, although that is not a feature of more recent discussions of his historiography.[122] Soon after Mallet's publication of the *Letters on History*, Birch reported that Sir George Lyttelton, once Bolingbroke's political ally, was writing 'a Confutation of his Ldp's [Bolingbroke's] Attack upon Sacred History, & even, according to another Account, to have actually printed twelve copies of it. But I have no good Authority, that he either has undertaken that subject, or intends to do it'.[123] Although Lyttelton never published anything like this, there were no fewer than seven publications in 1753 offering a vindication of the authenticity of the Gospels and sacred history.[124] Birch and Yorke assiduously followed the barrage of condemnation of Bolingbroke by Anglican divines, commenting at length on, for example, the *Vindication of the Histories of the Old and New Testament* written by Robert Clayton (1695–1758), the bishop of Clogher.[125] Birch's treatment of this book is a good example of his summarising practice, taking the source text seriously, offering a non-judgmental outline, allowing Yorke to draw his own conclusions, and seeming to abjure faction or doctrinal complexity. In his summary Birch told Yorke:

> The Bp's Vindication is an 8mo pamphlet of 140 pages & written with great Clearness, Learning, & Candour. He allows, that there are some small Additions, Interpolations, & Transpositions in the Sacred Writings of no consequence, which have been detected, & are daily detecting, as Learning increases in the World; but these are by no means of such purport, as to impeach the Truth & Credit of the Whole, or to prevent the Scripture from taking Effect with regard to the general Design of them: Nor does he think,

---

[121] BL: Add MS 35398: Birch to Yorke, 6 October 1753, ff. 170–1 (170r).
[122] Recent discussions of Bolingbroke's historiography have a concern with his discussion of historical evidence in ancient history, but have not been animated by his remarks on the authenticity of the Gospels and the authority of sacred history. See Nadel, 'New light', and Womersley, 'Bolingbroke and . . . historiography'.
[123] BL: Add MS 35398: Birch to Yorke, 30 September 1752, ff. 97–9 (97v).
[124] Vindications of sacred history published in response by Anglican controversialist divines: Robert Clayton (1695–1758, Bishop of Clogher), Abraham Le Moine (*d.* 1757), Richard Smyth, James Hervey (1714–58), John Leland (1691–1766), Peter Whalley (1722–91), with two anonymous pamphlets, and another by Alexander Campbell, a midshipman. There was also a defence of Bolingbroke by Caleb Fleming, a presbyterian Dissenting minister in London.
[125] BL: Add MS 35398: Birch to Yorke, 18 November 1752, ff. 112–13 (113r).

that all the Books, which are in the canon of the Jewish & Christian Scriptures, or all the passages in the same Book, are to be put upon a Level. He acknowledges likewise, that Dr Middleton's Argument, tho' he may have push'd it with too much Violence, & have gone too far in some particulars, is undeniably right in general. He mentions some other Letters of his, drawn up for the use of the young nobleman, to whom his Book is addres'd, as a philosophical Vindication of the Mosaical Account of the Creation & Deluge, which he intends to give the World, as a proper Sequel to his present Treatise.[126]

The subsequent letters noted by Birch here, published in 1757, adopted an extreme Arianism that itself attracted controversy.[127] Birch also commented at length on Warburton's reply to Bolingbroke's *Works*, published in 1754 as *A View of Lord Bolingbroke's Philosophy*.[128] Although anonymous, Birch told Yorke that it 'shews the hand of Dr. Warburton in every page'.

> The performance is, I sincerely think, a very good one, tho' the Wit is too often indelicate, & the language defective in correctness & purity. Pope's excess of admiration of Lord Bolingbroke is gently raillied; & a saying of his is recorded, that his Ldp was a superior Being, who did not originally belong to this system of ours; & when the last Comet appear'd, & came pretty near the Earth, Mr. Pope us'd to tell his acquaintance, that he should not be surprized, if in the Event it proved, that it was sent only to convoy his Ldp home again.[129]

Birch's wariness around Warburton's combative style can be seen here, even when he is enjoying the satirical smear of Bolingbroke and Pope.

The Bolingbroke controversy reached a climax in 1754 when his *Philosophical Works* were tried by the Grand Jury of Westminster for 'the subversion of religion government and morality and being against his Majesty's peace'. David Mallet was named as editor and Dr Morris of Stableyard, Rider Street, Westminster, as publisher.[130] Birch reported on the presentment of the case, the legal document laid before the Grand Jury. 'The noble sceptic would perhaps have felt some mortification if he could have forgotten this Insult offer'd to his memory by Toothdrawers, Taylors and Peruke-Makers; tho' after all he may be oblig'd to them for taking the office of censuring the Writings out of more considerable Hands.'[131] Yorke signalled his approval of the prosecution in his reply: 'I think any Man must carry his notions of the

---

[126] BL: Add MS 35398: Birch to Yorke, 18 November 1752, ff. 112–13 (113r–v).
[127] Leighton, 'Enlightened religion of Robert Clayton'.
[128] BL: Add MS 35398: Birch to Yorke, 3 November 1753, ff. 180–1.
[129] BL: Add MS 35398: Birch to Yorke, 5 October 1754, ff. 220–1 (221r).
[130] *A charge delivered to the Grand Jury* (1754), pp. 43–4.
[131] BL: Add MS 35398: Birch to Yorke, 26 October 1754, ff. 237–9 (238r, 239v).

Liberty of the Press to very great length indeed who should object to the Prosecution of a Book in wch the foundation of all Religion natural as well as revealed is openly attacked.'[132]

The curiosity Birch and Yorke showed in the activities and publications of François-Marie Arouet de Voltaire (FRS, 1694–1778) came from a similar place to their interest in Bolingbroke: an emotionally complex fascination with and rejection of his sceptical and controversial Deism. Voltaire's tempestuous sojourn in Berlin in the period from 1750 to 1753, as the guest of the philosopher-king Frederick of Prussia, generated both scandalous gossip and a prodigious number of texts, attracting the attention of Birch and especially Yorke.[133] Voltaire's personal notoriety reinforced their sense that he was the most significant contemporary foreign writer, as a poet, dramatist, historian, *philosophe* and polemicist, especially as he was also a Fellow of the Royal Society and corresponded with Sloane, Folkes and Maty. Yorke was a careful and engaged reader of Voltaire, more than any other philosopher. Voltaire's residence in Berlin saw the publication of several important works, eagerly sourced and consumed by both Birch and Yorke. The first was his new drama, *Rome Sauvée*, also known as *Catiline*, written in Paris in 1749 and performed in 1751.[134] Yorke was an enthusiastic critic, stating to Birch that 'I have read Voltaires Rome sauveé printed at Berlin, & incorrectly I believe. It is not equal to Merope or Zaire, but superior to Crebillons Catiline.'[135] In Yorke's response, he thinks like a critic, comparing the play to other works by the same writer (and sniping about the quality of the edition), rather than as a historian, who might have considered Voltaire's treatment of Cicero and the Catiline conspiracy. Two weeks later, Yorke had changed his mind. 'Voltaire's Catiline does not answer to my Expectations, there are good Lines in it, but some Alterations in the story wch displeases, & the Characters not equally work'd up. I begin to think it is not so proper a subject for the stage as the Historian.'[136]

Voltaire's time in Berlin allowed him to publish his influential history, *Le Siècle de Louis XIV*, in 1751.[137] This was an important work of history-writing with an innovative and structural focus on social history and the cultural achievements of France under Louis XIV. It furthermore claimed to be based

---

[132] BL: Add MS 35398: Yorke to Birch, Wrest, 30 October 1754, ff. 240–1 (241r).

[133] For Voltaire's period in Berlin see Besterman, *Voltaire*, pp. 308–33, and Pearson, *Voltaire almighty*, pp. 213–35.

[134] Yorke compares *Rome sauvée* (1752) with Voltaire's other dramas (*La Mérope françoise* (1744); *Zayre* (1733)) and Crebillon's earlier version of the same story (*Catilina: tragédie*, 1749)).

[135] BL: Add MS 35398: Yorke to Birch, Wrest, 28 May 1752, ff. 45–6 (46r).

[136] BL: Add MS 35398: Yorke to Birch, Wrest, 10 June 1752, ff. 54–5 (54v).

[137] Voltaire, *Le siècle de Louis XIV* (Berlin: 1751).

on empirical evidence rather than hearsay and tradition. In its own self-representation, it was the kind of history of which the Hardwicke Circle approved (though, unlike Birch's own documentary history, it was also brilliantly synthesised and concisely written: where Birch preferred the document to speak, Voltaire summarised). Yorke probably read it in the winter of 1751–2, and, when he commented on 28 May 1752, he was assessing its reception: ' – They speak slightingly of his memoirs of Lewis 14th at Paris, but that does no credit to their Judgement or Impartiality.'[138] On 10 June, Yorke reported some recent gossip: 'Voltaire begins to talk of a new Edition of his Lewis 14 improved with additional Anecdotes, we shall never know when he has done with it, but whilst he continues to mend it, I shall continue to read.'[139]

When Voltaire published *Le Supplément au Siècle de Louis XIV* in 1753, it was an attack on one of his critics in Berlin, Laurent Angliviel de La Beaumelle (1726–73), with whom he had quarrelled. In September 1753, Birch reported on the complicated bibliographic challenge posed by the book.

> The third Volume of le Siecle de Louis XIV just imported by our French Booksellers is an 8vo of about 350 pages printed at the Hague, containing Voltaire's own Corrections & Additions in the Dresden Edition of his Works, & the Remarks of Mons. de la Beaumelle first published in the Franckfort Edition of le Siecle last year in three Tomes, & the occasional Observations of both Voltaire & Beaumelle by a critic, who assumes the Name of Marc Phrasendorp, & animadverts upon those Writers.[140]

Beaumelle had inserted false and offensive material into the Frankfurt edition of *Le siècle de Louis XIV*, accusing Voltaire of a wide variety of crimes.[141] Yorke expressed an interest in seeing this, having received 'from Holland the Dresden Edition of Voltaire's Siecle', which was without Beaumelle's scandalous insertions. 'I shd like to see the 3d vol: of the Hague Edit[ion].' Yorke added instructions to Birch about how he might send the book: 'My Ld will be in Town next week, & if you send it to [Lord Hardwicke's] Powis House abt Wednesday or Thursday it will come safe to me when he returns.'[142]

Voltaire's name was also kept in view through his publication of incendiary satirical verses he had written in Berlin. In July 1752, Birch had visited Lady Isabella 'Bell' Finch (1700–71), an influential lady of the bedchamber to Princess Amelia. She had shown him a copy of verses written by Voltaire 'to

---

[138] BL: Add MS 35398: Yorke to Birch, Wrest, 28 May 1752, ff. 45–6 (46r).

[139] BL: Add MS 35398: Yorke to Birch, Wrest, 10 June 1752, ff. 54–5 (55r).

[140] BL: Add MS 35398: Birch to Yorke, 15 September 1753, ff. 159–60 (159r–v). Voltaire, *Oeuvres de Mr. de Voltaire* (A Dresden: Chez George Conrad Walther Libraire du roi, 1748–54).

[141] Beaumelle and Voltaire, *Le siècle de Louis XIV. Nouvelle édition, augmentée par M. de La B*** [La Beaumelle]* (Frankfort, 1753).

[142] BL: Add MS 35398: Yorke to Birch, Wimpole, 20 September 1753, ff. 161–2 (162v).

the King of Prussia upon his allowing a Church to be built for the Roman Catholics at Berlin'. Finch promised him a copy: an intriguing example of manuscript dissemination using a female line of transmission. However, Yorke, who was taking the waters in Scarborough, had already received a copy, sent to him with his regular newsletter *à la main* from his Paris literary agent, the Rev. John Jeffreys.[143] Cardinal Quirini at the Vatican had asked Voltaire to write verses in favour of the proposed new Catholic cathedral in Berlin, but Voltaire instead had written an ironic satire attacking the plan, entitled 'Epitre de Monsieur de Voltaire au Cardinal Quirini'. Disseminated only by manuscript, it was later printed, with intentional malice, to embarrass Voltaire. A few weeks later, in August 1722, Birch encountered another 'new poem of Voltaire', shown to him by Edward Mason, secretary to William, Duke of Cumberland. Birch made a précis of the poem's argument for Yorke: 'It is an epistle to the King of Prussia to explode a remark of Pascal, that Kings are miserable Beings, when divested of the Pomp of their Courts, & alone; & to compliment his Prussian Majesty on his Employments in his privacies. The Deity to whom that King is compar'd or rather preferr'd is treated with no small Freedom by the Poet.'[144] The assiduous attention Birch and Yorke pay to these satires reflected their wide though officially clandestine dissemination around Europe.

Voltaire's departure from Berlin in the summer of 1753 and his arrest in Frankfurt were the topic of much newspaper discussion. Embroiled in rancorous disputes with Maupertius, the senior natural philosopher at Frederick's Academy, Voltaire requested permission to resign his positions at his court and to leave Berlin. Travelling to Paris with his niece and lover, Marie Louise Mignot Denis (1712–90), Voltaire was detained in Frankfurt and held for several weeks. The London press reported Voltaire's movements, arrest and humiliation in early July. To advertise his predicament, Voltaire published supposedly private letters that explained his situation.[145] Birch reported to Yorke that Jean-Henri-Samuel Formey (1711–97), FRS, Secretary of the Academy of Sciences at Berlin, had suggested Voltaire's intention was to return to Paris and his French pensions. Birch added a gossipy tidbit that 'Voltaire himself in a Letter to Sr Evarard Falkenor from Germany mentions an Intention of his to pay another Visit to England.'[146] Sir Everard Fawkener (1694–1758)

---

[143] BL: Add MS 35398: Yorke to Birch, Scarborough, 26 July 1752, ff. 73–4 (75r–v).

[144] BL: Add MS 35398: Birch to Yorke, 22 August 1752, ff. 83–4 (84v). Voltaire, *Epître au roi de Prusse* (1751).

[145] *London Evening Post*, 7 July 1753; *London Magazine*, November 1753, 581–6; *Gentleman's Magazine*, November 1753, 505–8.

[146] BL: Add MS 35398: Birch to Yorke, 11 August 1753, ff. 145–6 (146v).

was an English merchant and diplomat who, having met Voltaire in Paris in 1725, had hosted his celebrated visit to England from 1726 to 1728 at his house in Wandsworth. A letter from Voltaire to Madame Denis, dated from Mayence 9 July 1753, gained notoriety in the press, as Voltaire intended. Birch wrote on 18 August with some excitement that

> A Letter of Voltaire to Madam St Dennis his Niece begins to be handed about here, tho' it has not yet reach'd me. Mr Wray who had an Account of it at the same time with myself has perhaps already anticipated the little, which I can remember of its contents; but I shall set down what I recollect, which will enable him to supply the rest.[147]

The letter was something of a hot property, not only an insight into the scandalous private life of the celebrated *philosophe*, but also an explicit denunciation of his treatment in Frankfurt and, by extension, the king of Prussia. Birch's scoop was not long-lasting, though: a few days after receiving this letter, Yorke replied that he had already received a copy of Voltaire's letter from Jeffreys in the Paris *à la main*.[148] Competition for Voltaire gossip was international and intense. Nonetheless, Birch gave a thorough précis of Voltaire's letter, using some of Voltaire's own rhetorical flourishes, as later published in the newspapers in November 1753 and appended to the satire *Babouc* in 1754. Birch comments on the 'Sufferings' that 'Madam St Dennis his Niece . . . was made to bear on his Account; to be siz'd & dragg'd away, & confin'd in the Strictest manner, without the Attendance of her Maid servant, & with one of the meanest officers of Justice'.[149] Voltaire's difficulties, especially those caused by his attempt to change allegiance from Louis to Frederick – from autocratic France to supposedly tolerant Prussia – and back again greatly entertained them. Birch and Yorke's curiosity about Voltaire, like their interest in Bolingbroke, shows their keen and somewhat prurient interest in scandal and gossip, but also reveals their considered interest in moral philosophy, Enlightenment historiography and religious toleration.

4.3 The Novel: Richardson, Smollett and Hill

This case study explores Birch and Yorke's taste for reading novels, a contentious genre that divided their attention and tested their loyalties. As Table 2 suggests, that section of *Belles lettres* comprising imaginative writing, including poetry, fiction, satires and plays, was a significant element of their reading (10 per cent). Perhaps unusually for this period, they preferred the term

---

[147] BL: Add MS 35398: Birch to Yorke, 18 August 1753, ff. 147–8 (148r).
[148] BL: Add MS 35398: Yorke to Birch, Wrest, 23 August 1753, ff. 149–50 (149r).
[149] BL: Add MS 35398: Birch to Yorke, 18 August 1753, ff. 147–8 (148r–v).

'novel' for prose fictions, although they also used 'adventure' and 'romance'. Their determination that fiction should be understood in a moral dimension implied that for them it was also political. Birch divided the category of fiction into that which was of a good tendency, which for him meant Richardson, and that which was not, which primarily meant Tobias Smollett and John Hill. In making this determination, Birch leaned on the distinctions made about the novel by Richardson and Fielding in the late 1740s. Birch and Yorke expressed a particular dislike for both prose satire and fiction that they considered vulgar or popular. Birch, on occasion, even borrowed Fielding's critical nomenclature, using the term a 'low kind' of tale to describe novels that follow, in the mode of Daniel Defoe, the story of an individual in low life.[150] As William Warner argued in *Licensing Entertainment*, Richardson and Fielding debated between themselves the nature of the moral novel while being united about the need to suppress those forms of licentious satirical prose fiction prevalent in earlier decades, especially those associated with scandalous women writers. Birch allied himself with this attitude in September 1750 when he remarked, 'Our own Country & Ireland have lost two of its Female Authors, Mrs Pilkington having drunk herself to Death at Dublin, & Mrs Phillips transported herself to Barbados.' He also noticed here 'Mrs Eliza Heywood, who is a much more harmless Writer than the other two, notwithstanding her Novels & Romances of no very edifying a Tendency'.[151] Birch's misogynist distaste for these women novelists – Laetitia Pilkington (1712–50), Teresia Constantia Phillips (1709–65) and Eliza Haywood (1693–1756) – also condemns their characteristic forms of quasi-biographical scandalous memoirs.[152]

The novelist for whom Birch and Yorke expressed the most enthusiasm was Samuel Richardson. Birch knew Richardson well as the printer of *Philosophical Transactions*. Richardson shared Birch and Yorke's view of the reformative and improving role of culture in the modern state. Richardson had had a major success with his novels *Pamela* and *Clarissa* in the 1740s, in which he had attempted, in his own view, to wrest the genre of the novel out of the hands of vulgar romance and adventure. His programme for a reformed moral novel continued in the 1750s with *Sir Charles Grandison*, a project to which Birch alerted Yorke as early as September 1750:

> Mr Richardson, the printer, is employing himself in a Work, for which the Men will be as much oblig'd to him, as the Ladies have hitherto been, having, as he own'd to me some days ago, resum'd the Subject, which you heard him mention at your own House, of the virtuous & generous Gentleman. He complains to me

---

[150] BL: Add MS 35397: Birch to Yorke, 10 November 1750, ff. 316–17 (317v).
[151] BL: Add MS 35397: Birch to Yorke, 15 September 1750, ff. 289–92.
[152] Thompson, *Scandalous Memoirists*.

of the Difficulty of enlivening it with proper Incidents: But we may safely trust to his Invention, which is inexhaustible upon all Occasions.[153]

Birch was one of the many friends of Richardson asked to give advice about the development of the novel's plot. 'He has desir'd me to give him an Hour or two's attention in the reading of his plan.'[154] Richardson's difficulty, in a story about a fully 'virtuous & generous Gentleman', was how to develop plot points that would engage the reader. Two years later, in November 1752, Birch announced that Richardson had 'brought to a conclusion his new Romance' and was in the process of publishing it. On 7 July 1753, Birch reported that Richardson, 'that ingenious Author', had read aloud to him sections of the book, including the preface, which 'recapitulates the different Designs of Pamela & Clarissa, & describes that of his present Work; & in the latter he justifies the perfection of some of his Characters from the Objections of those who represent them as too good to be at all copied in real Life'.[155] Birch commented that he had seen the size of the manuscript and believed the published work had 'been much abridg'd to bring it within the compass of ordinary Readers'.[156] Richardson published the first four volumes of *Sir Charles Grandison* in November 1753, the next two in December 1753 and the seventh in March 1754.[157]

Richardson was also concerned that his novel had been the subject of a concerted plagiarism plot. In 1752, Birch reported that he was 'under some Apprehensions of being anticipated by some hastier writer, who seems to have stolen his plan & story & even the names of the chief persons, & has offered his Manuscript to Millar, among other Booksellers'.[158] This publication, *Memoirs of Sir Charles Goodville*, probably by the actor Henry Giffard (1694–1772), was published on 20 February 1753: like *Grandison*, it was epistolary and explored the problem of a principal male character of 'Honour and Benevolence'.[159] Birch and Yorke, however, were more exercised by Richardson's separate discovery of an attempt by Dublin publishers to publish a piratical edition of the novel, which Birch thought was a 'monstrous Invasion of Literary property'.[160] Birch related that Richardson had discovered 'a gross

---

[153] BL: Add MS 35397: Birch to Yorke, 29 September 1750, ff. 298–9 (299v).
[154] BL: Add MS 35397: Birch to Yorke, 29 September 1750, ff. 298–9 (299v). On Richardson's revision coterie see Schellenberg, *Literary coteries*, 44–66.
[155] BL: Add MS 35398: Birch to Yorke, 7 July 1753, ff. 128–9.
[156] BL: Add MS 35398: Birch to Yorke, 7 July 1753, ff. 128–9.
[157] Eaves and Kimpel, *Richardson*, pp. 377–88.
[158] BL: Add MS 35398: Birch to Yorke, 18 November 1752, ff. 112–13 (113v).
[159] *Memoirs of Sir Charles Goodville* (1753). Giffard is identified as the author in Burditt, 'Authorship of . . . *Sir Charles Goodville*', pp. 406–7.
[160] BL: Add MS 35398: Birch to Yorke, 27 October 1753, ff. 178–9 (179r).

Instance of Infidelity' among the men of his own print shop who had sold proof sheets of his novel to the publishers in Dublin. 'The printed sheets' of his novel, Birch reported, had 'been immediately sent clandestinely to Dublin, where the press is almost as forward with all the Volumes as his own; by which Means he will lose 70 guineas, which Faulkner had agreed to allow him for his permission to reprint the Work'.[161]

Four Dublin publishers were involved in the conspiracy, the events of which Richardson summarised in a pamphlet entitled *An Address to the Public, on the Treatment which the Editor of the History of Sir Charles Grandison has met with from certain Booksellers and Printers in Dublin.* Birch later reported on Richardson's prosecution of Faulkner, who had the rights to Richardson's authorised edition, but, implicated in the 'piratical Edition', tried to persuade Richardson to sanction the Dublin edition. Richardson refused and pursued the matter through the courts, 'to secure to Authors the Benefit of their own Labours'.[162] Yorke was one of many in London who thought Richardson had little hope of winning his case, opining that 'All good men must be sorry for Mr Richardson's Misfortune, [but] I suppose ye Law will give no redress agst ye Corruption of ye Servants.'[163] Birch replied on 27 October 1753 that Richardson, despite 'some Overtures from Faulkner the Printer of Dublin', was: 'trying Measures to defeat the success of this monstrous Invasion of Literary property, & to Secure to himself the Emoluments of his own Edition in Ireland. This occasions him to suspend for some time the publication of the two first Volumes of his Work, which however he has presented me with'.[164]

Richardson gave Birch the first two volumes of *Grandison* several weeks before their publication. 'I have now read them over with as little Interruption as my Employments would permit; & think it a wonderful performance for Invention, Characters, & Morality, & superior in style, Sentiments & Manners to his *Clarissa*.'[165] Birch's enthusiasm for *Grandison* was not shared by every reader: in a very long novel about a good and virtuous man, Richardson had not solved the problem of a compelling plot, and while the book was technically well executed, some readers complained that it was dull and sanctimonious. It is perhaps telling that the section of which Birch took the most notice was Harriet Byron's attack on the 'dirty Imagination' of Swift, a comment Birch quoted to Yorke:

> He has had the Courage to put into the Mouth of Miss Harriot Byron a just censure upon Dr. Swift's writings, which I will particularly thank him for.

[161] BL: Add MS 35398: Birch to Yorke, 25 August 1753, ff. 151–2 (152v).
[162] Richardson, *Address to the public*, pp. 2, 3.
[163] BL: Add MS 35398: Yorke to Birch, Wimpole, 4 October 1753, ff. 168–9.
[164] BL: Add MS 35398: Birch to Yorke, 27 October 1753, f. 179r.
[165] BL: Add MS 35398: Birch to Yorke, 27 October 1753, ff. 179r–v.

This Lady, who is his principal Heroine, after remarking that <u>Wickedness &
Libertinism</u> are call'd a <u>Knowledge of the World</u>, & of <u>human Nature</u>, adds,
that Swift, for <u>often painting a Dunghill</u>, & for his <u>abominable Yahoo story</u>, was
complimented with this Knowledge. 'But I hope says she that the Character of
Human Nature, the Character of Creatures made in the Image of the Deity, is
not to be taken from the overflowings of such Dirty Imaginations.'[166]

Birch rarely quotes from a novel, so co-opting Richardson's attack on Swift is
arguably a significant indication of his cultural politics, notably his condemnation of vulgar satire. Birch had expressed hostility to Swift elsewhere: for
example, he welcomed Lord Orrery's very critical assessment of Swift's character in his biography published in 1752.[167] By contrast, Birch admired
Richardson's concern for propriety and politeness in imaginative literature,
and his project to reform the novel.

Those writers who did not follow these cultural prescriptions, especially the
satirical novelists Tobias Smollett (1721–71) and John Hill (1714?–75), met with
serious condemnation. Smollett offended, not only because he was a Tory, but also
because he practised as a quack physician. In November 1750, Birch reported that
Smollett was 'printing another set of Adventures, which, I presume, are of the <u>low</u>
Kind, if Mr Fielding will allow me the Use of that Word; for the name of the Hero
of the new piece is <u>Jeremiah Pickle</u>'.[168] Birch thought Smollett's *The Adventures of
Peregrine Pickle*, published in 1751, had met with such 'ill success' that it had
'ruin'd his Reputation among the Booksellers'. Nevertheless, Birch reported that
Smollett was 'trying his Fortune again as a Writer of Romances', with a novel,
Roderick Random (1752), in which a 'large share of Invective' was directed at
Birch's allies Sir George Lyttelton and the bookseller Andrew Millar, 'who has
particularly offended him by refusing to have any more concern with him'.[169]

Personal attacks on writers close to their circle incited reciprocal hostility. In
this vein, Birch also noted the appearance 'in the press' of the work of another
Tory satirical novelist, John Shebbeare (1709–88), whose novel *The Marriage
Act* (1754) Birch described as 'a Romance intended to expose the Consequences'
of Lord Hardwicke's Marriage Act of 1753 (26 Geo. II. c. 33).[170] Yorke and Birch
debated the novel's prosecution for libel. They noted it had been called in just

---

[166] BL: Add MS 35398: Birch to Yorke, 27 October 1753, ff. 179r–v; Richardson, *Sir Charles
Grandison* (1753–4), II, 89.
[167] BL: Add MS 35398: Birch to Yorke, 7 September 1751, ff. 26–7. Boyle, earl of Orrery, *Remarks
on Swift*.
[168] BL: Add MS 35397: Birch to Yorke, 10 November 1750, ff. 316–17 (317v). Smollett,
Adventures of Pickle (1751).
[169] BL: Add MS 35398: Birch to Yorke, 14 October 1752, ff. 104–5, (105r–v). Smollett, *Ferdinand
Count Fathom* (1753). Lyttelton appeared under the name Sir Gosling Scrag.
[170] BL: Add MS 35398: Birch to Yorke, 14 September 1754, ff. 210–11 (211v); Shebbeare,
Marriage act (1754).

after publication, that the printer, Hodges, was being prosecuted 'on account of the great Invectives upon the whole conduct of the Administration in the Close of it'. Birch added that Lord Hardwicke had a 'considerable share of the Scurrilities in this Libel' and that it was dedicated to the Duke of Bedford, whom Newcastle and Hardwicke had forced into opposition in 1751.[171] Birch associated these satirists with both Tory politics and low romance; his enthusiasm for the prosecution manifests his Court Whig cultural values.

Birch expressed a different kind of hostility to the 'inexhaustible' John Hill when, in July 1751, he read *The Adventures of Mr George Edwards, a Creole*.[172] Hill had already launched a series of devastating satires against the Royal Society in the period 1748–52. Birch complained that 'every page' of the new novel was 'full of personal Scandal', some of which was targeted at colleagues at the Royal Society, notably President Martin Folkes and Secretary Dr Cromwell Mortimer. Birch was also scandalised that 'There are whole chapters that abuse the workings of the Royal Society,' including 'gross Misrepresentations' about the publication of *Philosophical Transactions*.[173] Birch clearly read the novel attentively, decoding for Yorke the names of the characters in Hill's satire: 'Dr Mortimer', he said, 'appears under the title of Dr Single Dose, as pretending to cure all Diseases by a single Nostrum'. He also recalled that Hill's earlier novel *The Adventures of Mr. Loveill* (1750) had attacked Folkes's daughter.[174] The scandal of Hill's fiction was especially hurtful because it was personal, close to Birch, and tellingly accurate. Birch's condemnation paid close attention to Hill's novel, which had successfully integrated Hill's critique of the Royal Society's scientific programme into a novelistic satire.

5 Science, the Royal Society and Learned Journals

5.1 Natural Philosophy Publications

In the early 1750s, as has been shown, Birch was elected Secretary of the Royal Society, and Yorke was elected to its Council. They expressed native curiosity about natural philosophy: 136 reading events (16 per cent) concern publications firmly identifiable as natural history, although these engender a small amount of discussion. Birch and Yorke were mostly uninterested in experimental science, although the Weekly Letter records their attendance at a small number of scientific demonstrations. Instead, the focus of their attention in this area is

---

[171] BL: Add MS 35398: Birch to Yorke, 2 November 1754, ff. 242r–243v.
[172] Hill, *Adventures of George Edwards* (1751).
[173] BL: Add MS 35398: Birch to Yorke, 20 July 1751, ff. 12–13 (13r–v). Birch's comments on the list of persons at the club are quoted from Hill, *Edwards*, p. 163.
[174] Hill, *Adventures of Mr. Loveill* (1750).

the activities, politics and institutional demands of the Royal Society, the production and politics of *Philosophical Transactions* and their competitive curiosity about European learned institutions and their journals. These interests reflect their self-conscious mission to undertake institutional reforms in the Royal Society, especially with regard to its publication programme.

Birch's interest in scientific publications was often focussed on the scholarly scandal they aroused. In 1752, he noted 'a new piece' 'in favour of Cartesianism' by Bernard Le Bovier de Fontenelle (1657–1757) published anonymously in Paris. Birch found the book on a visit to Vaillant's French bookshop on The Strand. Fontenelle, aged ninety-five and still a figure of considerable prestige, was a former Secretary of the Académie des Sciences. Birch described the book to Yorke as 'a Theory of the Cartesian Vortices, with reflections upon Attraction'.[175] Fontenelle's book was a patriotic and late defence of the French Cartesian physics of vortices against the English Newtonian principles of gravitation. Leonard Marsak, a Fontenelle scholar, concludes that it is the 'clearest expression' of Cartesian principles 'when for all practical purposes Cartesianism was already dead in France'.[176] Writing to Yorke, however, Birch is more interested in the scandal surrounding its publication. Fontenelle had published it anonymously, but his name had been exposed by a rival Newtonian, Louis Godin, who 'thought he knew the Hand of that elegant Writer even on that serious Subject'. Godin observed, said Birch,

> that as it had been the good fortune of Des Carte's Philosophy to have very able Defenders, according to the Observation of a great Writer, this Book was so strong an Instance of the truth of that Remark, that he could not but suspect the Author of both to be the same person. Fontenelle pleas'd with the Conjecture of Monsr Godin, & his manner of expressing it, avow'd his performance to him.

Birch learned of this anecdote from the editor's preface by Falconet, 'a Man likewise between eighty & ninety'.[177] Although he showed little interest in Cartesian vortices, Birch enjoyed this anecdote not only for its polite and elegant wit, but also for its revelations of rivalry and scandal within the Paris academy.

In his role as Secretary of the Royal Society, Birch received correspondence, including packets of books and pamphlets, from *philosophes* around Europe, gifts that were both unsolicited and *ex officio*. These presentation copies and correspondence from the officers of foreign academies came freighted with

---

[175] BL: Add MS 35398: Birch to Yorke, 27 June 1752, ff. 60–1; Fontenelle, *Théorie des tourbillons cartésiens* (1752).

[176] Marsak, 'Cartesianism in Fontenelle', p. 51. See also Shank, *The Newton wars*.

[177] BL: Add MS 35398: Birch to Yorke, 27 June 1752, ff. 60–1 (61r).

distinctive prestige and obligations that provided material for the Weekly Letter. In 1751, Birch noted that 'Mons Reaumur has sent over copies of his new treatise upon hatching of eggs, with notes of the ostrich not abandoning their eggs except during the heat of the day.'[178] René Antoine Ferchault de Réaumur (1683–1757) had been a member of the Académie des Sciences since 1708 and an FRS since 1738, noted especially for his work on insects and for his wide-ranging work in physics and mechanics. In the volume gifted to Birch, Réaumur set out a system for artificially maintaining fertilised eggs at a constant warmth so as to bring them to hatch – as well as correcting a widely reported fallacy about ostriches. In 1752, Birch carried a letter from Réaumur (aged sixty-nine) to Sir Hans Sloane (aged ninety-two) in Chelsea. There Birch found Sloane was 'chearfull & healthfull, but is almost incapable of conversation from his Defects of hearing and speech'. The letter from Réaumur 'compliments him upon his very advanc'd Age, as having effectually [negated] the greatest Blot upon his profession, that of a short Life'.[179]

In 1752 and 1754, Birch received letters from the Jesuit mission in Beijing. The first packet in 1752, addressed to the already deceased former secretary Cromwell Mortimer, contained five letters from Father Jean Sylvain de Neuvialle in Macau and Father Antoine Gaubil of the French House in Peking. Birch commented to Yorke that they 'promise me a good Correspondence with that Country, which I am resolv'd to cultivate'. The obligations of letters as gifts flowed both ways, of course. With these letters came a twenty-four-volume Notitia (register) of Chinese history and 'a Box of Curiosities of the Country, which I shall endeavour immediately to get into my Hands'. Gaubil promised some explanatory notes on the Notitia, 'which is unfortunately in the Chinese language', and also to send next year 'a Plan of Peking', 'with a Chinese Planisphere, & if possible, a Vocabulary'.[180] Birch replied on 11 October 1752, but his mail took so long to arrive in China that the French missionaries received his reply only a week before they had planned to send their next packet, which contained two letters from Pierre Nicolas Le Chéron d'Incarville dated 25 October and 14 November 1753, still directed to Dr Mortimer, and one in Latin from Father Gaubil to Birch, dated 23 November 1753, with further examples of Chinese artifacts. Birch commented enthusiastically on some silk paintings of the emperor's palace 'done by a young Painter, who attends Father d'Incarville to the Palace as his Servant, & by that means has an opportunity of drawing whatever is most remarkable there'. Gaubil's letter made a request for flower seeds and bulbs sourced from

---

[178] BL: Add MS 35398: Birch to Yorke, 7 September 1751, ff. 26–7 (27r).
[179] BL: Add MS 35398: Birch to Yorke, 27 June 1752, ff. 60–1.
[180] BL: Add MS 35398: Birch to Yorke, 1 August 1752, ff. 77–8 (78v).

the directors of the botanical gardens at Edinburgh, Chelsea and Oxford, which they might use as a gift to the Qianlong emperor, who usually had no relish for European productions of any kind. As Birch commented: 'The Emperor condescends to desire the Flowers & Legumes of Europe, & was highly pleas'd with the Sensitive Plant presented to him last year by Father d'Incarville.'[181] Yorke replied to this news with typical self-absorption by asking Birch to request from the missionaries 'a Chinese Gazette [newspaper] with a Translation, for that piece of scant Service, if it puts the good Fathers to any Expence, I will be answerable'.[182] Despite the extended postal delay occasioned by such distances, Birch's Beijing correspondence confirmed for him the global reach of the republic of letters.[183]

In 1754, Birch also received communications from the *philosophes* in Paris. From Jean-Jacques d'Ortous de Mairan (1678–1771), who had served as Secretary of the Académie des Sciences from 1740–3, after Fontenelle, he received a copy of the second edition of his work on astronomy, *Traité physique et historique de l'aurore boréale*, which had first been published in 1731 (and which had led to his election as FRS in 1735). Birch noted the title and added the comment that the second edition's 'Eclaircissements' amounted 'to near half the book'.[184] In the same letter, Birch also recorded that he had received three copies of the Abbé Guillaume-Thomas Raynal's latest book, *Mémoires historiques, militaires et politiques de l'Europe*, which had been promised when Raynal was elected FRS in July of that year.[185] Birch noted that these gifts had specific addressees: 'one for the Royal Society, another for your Lordship, which I have sent to St James's Square, & the third for my self'.[186] Receiving these gifts not only reflected on the prestige of Birch's position, but also recognised Yorke's importance within the Royal Society. Correspondence with European *philosophes* was a hallmark of a networked Republic of Letters, and also an occasion for rivalry and point-scoring. Birch and Yorke felt the competition with these international rivals keenly.

---

[181]   BL: Add MS 35398: Birch to Yorke, 21 September 1754, ff. 214–15 (214v–215r).

[182]   BL: Add MS 35398: Yorke to Birch, Wimpole, 1 October 1754, ff. 218–19 (218v).

[183]   One of these letters was published by the Royal Society: D'Incarville, 'Letter from Father D'Incarville', *Philosophical Transactions* 48 (1753–4), 253–60. The remaining letters were archived: BL: Add MS 4439: Antoine Gaubil and Pierre d'Incarville, to Dr. C. Mortimer, 30 October 1751–2 November 1752, ff. 190–4, 197–204b; BL: Add MS 4308: Antoine Gaubil, SJ to Cromwell Mortimer, ff. 47–65; BL: Add MS 4315: de Neuvialle, SJ to Birch, ff. 214–17. Two letters from Gaubil (dated 30 October 1751 and 6 November 1651) were read to the meeting of the Royal Society on Thursday, 1 March 1753 (Royal Society: Journal Book Original, JBO/22, pp. 281–2).

[184]   BL: Add MS 35398: Birch to Yorke, 21 September 1754, ff. 214–15 (215r).

[185]   BL: Add MS 35398: Birch to Yorke, 13 July 1754, ff. 186–9.

[186]   BL: Add MS 35398: Birch to Yorke, 21 September 1754, ff. 214–15 (215r).

5.2 Learned Journals in the Weekly Letter

Both Birch and Yorke took considerable interest in learned journals. From January 1752, on Birch's accession to the post of Secretary of the Royal Society, Birch was responsible for the collation and publication of *Philosophical Transactions*, although his concern about the publication was developed well before that. Cromwell Mortimer's final number of the *Transactions*, No. 497, was 'printed off just before his Death on the 7th of January 1752'.[187] On 20 June 1752, Birch wrote in the Weekly Letter that he had sent his first issue, the first part of volume 47, off to the press:

> The new Volume of the Phil. Transactions was put to the Press on Monday, & the Impression will proceed at the rate of three Sheets a Week on a new Letter & better paper than what has been us'd in the former Volume's. I shall have the more leisure to attend to this as the Society adjourn'd on Thursday for near five Months till Novemb. the 9th.[188]

Under Birch's management, the publication was contracted to Birch's old acquaintance, Samuel Richardson, the novelist and printer.[189] Birch, showing his tacit knowledge of publishing, told Yorke that Richardson would use a newly cut font, or 'new Letter', and print on a higher quality 'better paper' (Figure 12).[190] Having been elected to improve the administrative and professional functions of the Royal Society, Birch made these improvements among his first actions.

A sense of administrative crisis in the Royal Society was suddenly brought to the fore, however, by a letter Yorke received from his correspondent in Paris, the Rev. John Jeffreys. In September 1752, Jeffreys wrote to Yorke that

> I think it is my duty to acquaint you that I have lately had another Academical complaint against our R Society, they have long expected a Present of your Philosophical Transaction in return for their Memoirs. I shall be glad to know whether the complaint has any foundation.[191]

The Rev. John Jeffreys (*d*. 1798) was the rector of St Nicholas, Cole-Abbey, London. He was appointed chaplain to the embassy to France under William

---

[187] *Philosophical Transactions* 46 (1749–50), note on the titlepage recto. As this suggests, the titlepage, contents and index for each volume were printed separately from the numbers and compiled at binding.

[188] BL: Add MS 35398: Birch to Yorke, 20 June 1752, ff. 52–3 (53r–v). Birch discontinued internal numbering of discrete parts of a volume: *Philosophical Transactions* No. 47 has one series of articles numbered I–XCVII.

[189] Sale, *Richardson: master printer*, 73–5.

[190] The font was Caslon in both, so Birch may mean a new-cut version on this. Any improvement in paper quality is not discernible after 220 years.

[191] BL: Add MS 35630: Jeffreys to Yorke, Paris, 5 September 1753, ff. 102–3 (102v).

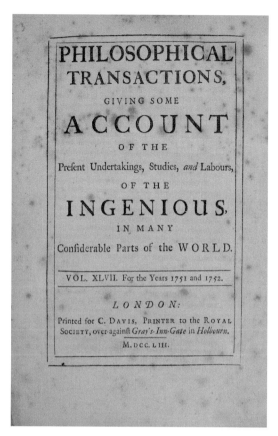

Figure 12 Titlepage, *Philosophical Transactions, Giving Some Account Of The Present Undertakings, Studies, And Labours Of The Ingenious, In Many Considerable Parts Of The World. Vol. XLVII. For The Years 1751 And 1752* (London: Printed for C. Davis, 1753), Royal Society Library.

Anne Keppel, second earl of Albemarle (1702–54), and resided in Paris from 1752 until the embassy was withdrawn in 1755. Yorke commissioned the 'Abbé Jeffreys' (as he called him) to be 'his library Chargé' in Paris.[192] Like Birch in London, Jeffreys scouted out literary and political information and acted as the go-between for Yorke's subscription to an underground commercial French *à la main* or scribal newsletter.[193] Jeffreys refers to the gift in July 1750 from the Paris Académie to the Royal Society of sixty-nine volumes of their annual 'Memoirs', the *Histoire de l'Academie Royale des Sciences. Avec les Memoires*

---

[192] BL: Add MS 35398: Yorke to Birch, Wimpole, 20 September 1751; BL: Add MS 35398, ff. 28–30.

[193] See Ellis, 'Yorke and Birch: scribal news', pp. 209–19.

de Mathematique et de Physique.[194] These volumes were a reprint of the official proceedings of the Académie des Sciences, edited by Jean Paul Grandjean de Fouchy, permanent secretary of the Académie des Sciences. Subsequent gifts of the most recent editions of the Académie's *Memoirs* were received in 1752.[195] For the Académie to have made a gift was prestigious, but for the Royal Society to have failed to reciprocate was embarrassing. Yorke wrote immediately to Birch.

> I shd be glad, you would enable me to answer an objection wch the Abbé Jeffreys has met wth at Paris, to the behaviour of our R. Society. viz. their long delay in returning the Present of the Academy of Sciences there with another of the like kind. – I thought as Ld Macclesfield had presented us wth one of his own Sets of the Transactions, that they wd have been immediately sent. The new binding of them, wch I presume was necessary, cd have taken up but a short time. – Some of their Members are not the best disposed towards us, & seem willing to cavil at Trifles.[196]

As Yorke explains, Lord Macclesfield, who had not yet been elected president of the Society, had provided a duplicate set of *Philosophical Transactions* from his own library, but it needed to be rebound, presumably to be both more uniform and more splendid in appearance, as appropriate for a diplomatic gift of this kind. Yorke was clearly unaware this had not yet happened. Two days later, in the Weekly Letter, Birch could report some progress:

> The arrival in Paris of the Philos. Transactions, now in their way thither, will soon silence the Reproaches of the Academicians there against the Ingratitude of our Society; as my Letter to their Secretary, sent with the Memoirs of Sr Hans Sloan, accounted for the Delay of those Transactions by the Difficulty of procuring several of the prints wanting in them.[197]

Birch reassured Yorke that the Society had responded to the gift and that the rebound set of the journal was en route. With it was sent Birch's 'Memoir of Sir Hans Sloane', a manuscript account of the ex-president's life translated into French: Grandjean de Fouchy replied with an eloge on Sloane.[198] The rivalry between the two institutions was polite, scholarly and personal, but can also be read in relation to the increasing geopolitical tensions between Britain and

---

[194] Royal Society, CMO/4, 4 July 1750, p. 33.

[195] Royal Society, JMO/22 Thursday, 5 March 1752, 69 (for the years 1746 and 1747) and JMO/22, 14 November 1754, 610 (for the year 1750).

[196] BL: Add MS 35398: Yorke to Birch, Wimpole, 20 September 1753, ff. 161–2 (161r–v).

[197] BL: Add MS 35398: Birch to Yorke, 22 September 1753, ff. 163–4 (163r).

[198] BL: Add 4241: Birch, 'Memoirs relating to the Life of Sr Hans Sloane Bart, 1753'. Birch's 'Memoir' is a manuscript in English (ff. 1–25), with a shorter version in French (ff. 26–35); BL: Add MS 4307: Jean Paul Grandjean de Fouchy to Birch, ff. 123–41; and BL: Add 4241: Fouchy, 'Éloge de M. Sloane' [printed with an autograph note addressed to Birch], ff. 38–46b.

France in the years before the Seven Years' War, also marked in the Weekly Letter.[199]

Birch and Yorke took a wide-ranging but by no means exhaustive interest in the learned journals of Europe. Their focus was, unsurprisingly, *Philosophical Transactions*, but they surveyed and followed a range of current journals from Germany, France and the Netherlands. The learned journal they followed most closely was Matthew Maty's *Journal Britannique* (nine reading events), whose purpose was to review British publications in literature, theology, history, geography and natural philosophy, so as to make them known to a wider European audience. It was accordingly published in French at The Hague in the Netherlands. Maty was a French Protestant who had studied medicine at Leiden, came to London in 1740 and was elected FRS in 1751. Maty was good friends with Birch and like him a recipient of Hardwicke patronage: he later became an under-librarian at the British Museum in 1756 and then secretary of the Royal Society after Birch in 1765. His collaborators included John Jortin, Jean Des Champs and César de Missy, as well as Birch. Maty initiated the sociable tea-drinking assembly of London philosophers known generically as Maty's Tea. This sociable gathering was a source of information for the Weekly Letter, as in September 1751, when Birch noted that Jortin had supplied Dr Maty with 'critical observations on the Classics, some of which are publish'd in the Journal Britannique for last month'.[200] Birch developed a distinctive reading practice for learned journals of this kind. He devoted a substantial paragraph, or even a whole page, to a list of the contents, giving a short title and including a summary of the contents in the form of a short and pithy description or abstract of the article or argument. These abstracts are too short to offer a proper summary of the article, but serve simply to identify the topic. The intention was to advertise to Yorke the contents of a journal which Yorke would later have the opportunity to read himself.[201]

Birch also took regular notice of issues he received of *Bibliothèque raisonnée des ouvrages des savans de l'Europe* (five reading events). This too was a commercial learned journal published by the well-known Amsterdam publishing house established by Johan Wetstein (1649–1726). The journal was edited by his grandson, Jacques Wetstein, from the company's large premises on Kalverstraat, Amsterdam. *Bibliothèque raisonnée* was a quarterly duodecimo of around 240 pages, comprising about fifteen articles in French on topics that ranged across theology and religion, law, history and natural

---

[199] See, for example, Houston, 'Franklin and the "Wagon Affair"', pp. 240–6.

[200] BL: Add MS 35398: Birch to Yorke, 21 September 1751, ff. 33–4 (34r).

[201] BL: Add MS 35398: Birch to Yorke, 11 August 1753, ff. 145–6 (146v); Add MS 35398: Birch to Yorke, 7 September 1754, ff. 208–9 (209v).

philosophy, usually taking the form of review discussions of recent publications, many of which were English. Established in 1728, it ended publication in 1753 after fifty volumes over twenty-five years.[202] In the Weekly Letter, Birch on three occasions brings news to Yorke of new issues. In July 1750, for example, when he writes to Yorke that 'The Bibliotheque Raisonée for January Febr & March contains an Extract of Bower's first Volume & Father Barre's Histoire generale d'Allemagne.' Of Barre's *Histoire* he says the journal offers 'some fine Criticisms upon that Work, which seems, from the specimen exhibited there, to abound with Error'.[203] Birch's treatment of *Bibliothèque Raisonée* followed the model he used with *Journal Britannique*: a list of articles identified by their short title or topic, together with a summarising phrase, adding up to about half a page of the letter, intended to advertise the contents to Yorke.[204] News of learned journals flowed between them. In October 1752, Birch wrote 'I have two Bibliotheque Germaniques & one Raisonée, to give you some Account of; but you will perhaps be more curious to see the Books themselves, which I will bring with me to Wrest.'[205] In 1753, Birch wrote with the disturbing news that Wetstein had decided to discontinue publication with the next issue, which would 'conclude the 50th Time & to be the close of the whole'.[206] Birch received this volume and an index in October 1753.[207]

Birch also followed *Nouvelle Bibliothèque Germanique* (four reading events), published in Amsterdam and edited by Jean-Henri-Samuel Formey (1711–97), perpetual secretary of the Royal Prussian Academy of Science. In November 1750, Yorke asked Birch if the latest edition 'contains anything remarkable, pray send me some Acct of it & most of the Books it contains, an Extract is as much as one shd desire to see'.[208] In his reply, Birch told Yorke that he had only recently managed to get it, and, in the next, he devoted half a page to summaries of both parts, in his customary way, listing titles and contents of key articles. The editor, Formey, had been elected FRS in 1750, with the rationale that 'Such a one as will be of great Service to us, by the

---

[202] See Lagarrigue, *L'histoire externe de la 'Bibliothèque raisonnée'*.

[203] BL: Add MS 35397: Birch to Yorke, 14 July 1750, ff. 261–2 (262r–v). Barre, *Histoire générale d'Allemagne* (1748).

[204] BL: Add MS 35398: Birch to Yorke, 20 June 1752, ff. 52–3 (53r); Add MS 35398: Birch to Yorke, 13 October 1753, ff. 172–3 (173v).

[205] BL: Add MS 35398: Birch to Yorke, 14 October 1752, ff. 104–5 (104r).

[206] BL: Add MS 35398: Birch to Yorke, 21 July 1753, ff. 136–7 (137r).

[207] BL: Add MS 35398: Birch to Yorke, 13 October 1753, ff. 172–3 (173v).

[208] BL: Add MS 35397: Yorke to Birch, Wrest, 1 November 1750, 312–13 (313r); *Nouvelle bibliothèque Germanique, ou Histoire litteraire de L'Allemagne, de la Suisse, & des pays du Nord* 6 (1750), parts 2 (April–June) and 3 (July–September).

ready disposition he is in, to keep up a correspondence between those Societies both founded for the advancement of the Same branches of usefull knowledge'.[209] Formey's journal, conducted in French and printed in Amsterdam, provided a useful summary view of 'the Acts of the Petersburg, Berlin & Copenhagen Academies', as Birch described it.[210] Birch exchanged letters and gifts with Formey in 1753, receiving a packet containing a volume of *Histoire de l'Academie royale des sciences et des belles lettres de Berlin,* the official journal of the Berlin academy, along with some of Formey's own essays, entitled *Mélanges philosophiques.*[211]

Around the time Wetstein decided to cease publication of *Bibliothèque Raisonée*, Maty told Birch that he was considering doing the same: 'Dr. Maty has likewise an Intention to quit the Journal Britannique as the end of the 12th Volume & the present Year, his application to it being inconsistent with his Health & the Duties of his Profession, & the Expence of purchasing Books for carrying it on to greater for the profit of the Sale to himself.'[212]

In fact, *Journal Britannique* limped on for another two years under the editorship of De Mauve. But having the two French-language journals that were known for a considered focus on British scholarship both cease publication was worrying, pointing to a crisis in learned journal publishing. Better news came in 1754 when Charles Chaix began publishing *Bibliothèque des Sciences et des Beaux-Arts* from The Hague (three reading events). Birch informed Yorke in October 1754 that 'I have at last procur'd the two first parts of the <u>Bibliotheque des Sciences et des Beaux Arts</u>, printed at the Hague.'[213] He summarised the 'chief articles' in his usual brief manner, which was enough to pique Yorke's interest. He replied, 'I should be glad to read over the new literary Journal wch you mention in your last, as some of the articles of it are new to me.'[214] Birch sent them, together with the most recent *Bibliothèque Germanique*, to his house in St James's.[215]

5.3 Royal Society Meetings As Reading Events

Birch also uses the Weekly Letter to record papers he had heard read at the weekly meetings of the Royal Society. As reading events, they have unusual and distinctive characteristics. With the president or one of the vice-presidents in the

---

[209] Royal Society EC/1749/19.
[210] BL: Add MS 35397: Birch to Yorke, 3 November 1750, 314–15 (315v); BL: Add MS 35397: Birch to Yorke, 10 November 1750, ff.316–17 (317r–v).
[211] BL: Add MS 35398: Birch to Yorke, 6 October 1753, ff. 170–1 (171v).
[212] BL: Add MS 35398: Birch to Yorke, 21 July 1753, ff. 136–7 (137r).
[213] BL: Add MS 35398: Birch to Yorke, 12 October 1754, ff. 222–3 (223v).
[214] BL: Add MS 35398: Yorke to Birch, Wrest, 15 October 1754, ff. 226–7 (227r).
[215] BL: Add MS 35398: Birch to Yorke, 19 October 1754, ff. 229–32 (229r).

Figure 13 John Arthur Quartley, 'A Meeting of the Royal Society in Crane Court', wood engraving, in Walter Thornbury, *Old and New London: A Narrative of Its History, Its People, and Its Places*. 2 vols. (Cassell, Petter & Galpin, London, 1878), Wellcome Collection, London, 23974i

chair, meetings at Crane Court were conducted by the secretaries (Daval and Mortimer, later Birch). The secretaries received epistolary communications from their correspondents, usually but not always fellows, and, at the meeting, read these letters aloud to the assembled fellows (as depicted in a nineteenth-century reimagining in Figure 13). Reading aloud in this manner had been established as a part of the Royal Society's practice since its early decades.[216] Discussion and debate followed the reading of the letter, sometimes accompanied by practical demonstrations of experimental knowledge or displays of material objects. Subsequently, the secretary made a record of the letter for the Journal Book, and after that, made a selection of the papers for publication in *Philosophical Transactions*. As such, they retained some of the markers of epistolary communication, including gentlemanly honorifics, and the addressee and signature conventions of the familiar letter. Persuaded by John Hill's devastating critique of the quality of the papers in his *Review of the Works of the Royal Society of London* (1751), many had come to believe that the secretaries, especially Mortimer, published anything and everything they had to hand, without judgement as to quality.[217] In Birch's election to the post of

---

[216] Anderson, 'Letters of Van Leeuwenhoek', p. 8.
[217] Hill, *Review of the works of the Royal Society* (1751).

secretary, much was made of his intention to reform *Philosophical Transactions* to remove these corruptions. His first volume was completed in June 1752.[218] The most significant of the reforms to *Philosophical Transactions* in 1752 was the decision of the Council to decide collectively on the papers to publish, in a new meeting called the Committee of Papers: in other words, to adopt a form of peer review. Macclesfield, Yorke and Birch were active in promoting the change, which was resisted by some fellows, who believed that it would leave the journal at the mercy of factions within the Royal Society.

Birch's habit of describing 'papers', 'letters' and 'accounts' read at the Royal Society in the Weekly Letter reiterates the significance of reading aloud in this process, though it is often omitted in treatments of how scientific papers were published.[219] Equally, analysis of the practice and theory of reading aloud in the eighteenth century does not consider the case of the Royal Society.[220] Birch's comments on the delivery of public lectures suggest that what he valued in reading aloud was 'a strong, clear, & lively Expression', or again, speakers that were 'elegant & unaffected'.[221] But reading scientific correspondence aloud differed from the elocutionary practices specified for sermons and political speeches or the experience of spouting clubs and elocution manuals.[222] Letters on scientific topics, particularly those on more abstract, mathematical or data-driven topics, must also have posed considerable problems to the secretary. Birch noted on one occasion how long he had read aloud: 'for the necessary Business before our Adjournment required of me an almost uninterrupted Course of reading of papers for an hour & three quarters'.[223] The imprint of sociable oral reading may be legible in the cadences and flow of some published pieces in *Philosophical Transactions.* The Royal Society's practice of reading aloud did not appeal to everyone. A satire published in 1777, entitled 'Philosophical Judgment' (see Figure 14), depicted the president, Sir John Pringle, reading aloud from a paper called 'Short on Grinding', while other papers, inscribed 'Natl History', 'Anatomy' and 'Nat. Philo[sophy]', litter the table. While reading is central to the meeting, the members who are listening are mostly asleep or yawning, except for an alert young clergyman to the president's left.

218 BL; Add MS 35398: Birch to Yorke, 20 June 1752, ff. 52–3 (53r–v).
219 For example, Moxham and Fyfe, 'Prehistory of peer review'; Banks, 'Publishing the research article', p. 10. Note that Moxham, Gielas and Fyfe consider the social contexts of reading aloud and the sociable practices of evaluation during Bank's presidency in '"Accoucheur of literature": Joseph Banks and the *Philosophical Transactions*', especially pages 28–9.
220 Mullini, 'Reading aloud in Britain'; Williams, *Social life of books.*
221 BL: Add MS 35397: Birch to Yorke, 26 August 1750, ff. 278–9 (279r); Add MS 35398: Birch to Yorke, 23 September 1752, ff. 93–4 (93v).
222 Goring, 'Elocutionary movement in Britain', 1–12; Bannet, 'History of reading', p. 123.
223 BL: Add MS 35398: Birch to Yorke, 6 July 1754, ff. 182–3 (183r–v).

Figure 14 'Philosophical judgment Decr I. 1777', etching, British Museum, Prints and Drawings, 1857,0520.309. © The Trustees of the British Museum

Twenty meetings of the Royal Society are reported in the Weekly Letter, including one of the Committee of Papers and one of the Council. These twenty meetings generate a total of fifty-three reading events. Typically, when reporting on these meetings, Birch does little more than list the titles of the papers, using a short form, in the order they were read, separated by semi-colons, following the practice he adopted for learned journals. Occasionally he makes a more considered intervention or judgement, of the kind discussed later in this section, mostly concerning natural history and antiquarian papers (and almost never concerning mathematical or physical ones). Yorke only once comments on these reading events, underlining his lack of interest in natural philosophy.

The appearance of the Royal Society meetings in the Weekly Letter follows a deceptively irregular pattern because Birch undertook the Weekly Letter only during the Long Vacation when Yorke was out of town, a timetable itself determined not only by the parliamentary session, but also the calendar of the Royal Society, which adjourned for summer between late June and mid-November, and returned for the annual meeting on St Andrews Day, 30 November, at which the Council for the next year was elected. As Table 7 shows, the weeks when the Weekly Letter overlapped with the term of the Royal Society varied considerably each year.

In 1750, Birch and Yorke had a curious discussion of ants and bees. It was engendered by a paper from Arthur Dobbs read at the Royal Society in November 1750 'containing his Remarks upon Bees', in which, as Birch observed, 'He differs from Monsr Reaumur in some points.'[224] Réaumur had been the acknowledged expert on insects since the publication of his six-volume *Mémoires pour servir à l'histoire des insects* (1734–42). Arthur Dobbs's letter, which was subsequently published in *Philosophical Transactions* for 1750, made a distinctive contribution as the first to observe the role of bees in pollination. Yorke replied a few days later, asking about bee matriarchy:

> As I know you are always awake at the Royal Society, I wish you wd recollect whether Mr Dobbs in his Paper about the Bees, confirmed the late system of the Naturalists, that the Queen is the Mother of the Hive, the Drones are her Seraglio, & the Working Bees neutrals. This Oeconomy if true is very remarkable. Mr Gould says much the same in his History of Ants.[225]

Yorke here recalls William Gould's recent entomology *An Account of English Ants* (1747), which promised to examine the 'many curiosities observable in these surprising Insects'. Birch replied a few days later that 'Monsr Reaumur's astonishing System of the Bees is justified in all the capital Articles by Mr Dobbs, who particularly agrees with him in the Nature & Qualities of the Queen Bee, &c.'[226] In his letter, Dobbs consistently acknowledges his debts to Réaumur, but Birch had failed to notice Dobbs's important and innovative observations about pollination and the production of beeswax.

Birch was more concerned by disputes amongst fellows of the Royal Society. In 1752, he followed the dispute between a group of working members, in this case, scientific-instrument makers, who were squabbling over the precedence of discoveries about a temperature-compensated clock pendulum. This addressed the problem that pendulum clocks run faster in cold winter weather than hotter

---

[224] BL: Add MS 35397: Birch to Yorke, 10 November 1750, ff. 316–17.
[225] BL: Add MS 35397: Birch to Yorke, 10 November 1750, f. 318v.
[226] BL: Add MS 35397: Birch to Yorke, 17 November 1750, ff. 320–1.

Table 7 Weekly Letter Reading Database: Royal Society meetings in the Weekly Letter 1750–1754

Year	Weekly Letter Annual Date Range	Parliamentary Long Vacation	Royal Society Meetings noted in Weekly Letter	Royal Society meetings in Weekly Letter	Reading events
1750	19 May to 17 Nov.	12 Apr. 1750 to 17 Jan. 1751	10 May, 17 May, 24 May, 31 May, 21 June 1 Nov, 8 Nov, 15 Nov	8	21
1751	29 June to 12 Oct.	25 June 1751 to 14 Nov. 1751	27 June	1	2
1752	23 May to 29 Nov.	26 Mar. 1752 to 11 Jan. 1753	14 May, 28 May, 4 June, 11 June, 18 June, 9 Nov, 16 Nov	7	26
1753	12 June to 3 Nov.	7 June 1753 to 15 Nov. 1753	21 June, 19 July (Council)	1	1
1754	6 July to 2 Nov.	Adjourned 5 June–14 Nov 1754[227]	4 July, 8 July (Committee of Papers)	2	4
				20	53

227 In 1754, an election year, Parliament was dissolved on 8 April 1754, before the election between 13 April 1754 and 20 May 1754. Parliament was recalled between 31 May 1754 and 5 June 1754 for the State Opening, and then was in recess over the Long Vacation until 14 November 1754.

summer weather.[228] Building on the observation that different metals expand at differing rates, the London clockmaker John Ellicot (FRS, 1706–72) published a description of a pyrometer, a mechanism for measuring these differences, in 1736, and returned to the topic in 1752 with a paper showing how this might be applied to pendulum design.[229] Birch noted that he read this at the Royal Society on 4 June 1752: 'I read likewise a long & curious Description of Mr Ellicott of two Methods, by which the irregularity of Rotation of a Clock arising from the Influence of Heat & Cold upon the Rod of the Pendulum may be prevented.'[230] Although Birch describes it as 'long & curious', his summary for Yorke essentially repeats the title of the paper as he recorded it in the Journal Book and as it was published in *Philosophical Transactions* for 1751–2.[231]

In September 1753, Birch noted that Ellicot's research was disputed by the telescope maker James Short, in a paper read at the Royal Society on 9 November 1752, and later published in *Philosophical Transactions*, in which Short provided an 'historical account' of temperature-compensated clock pendulums, showing that Ellicot's solution had first been theorised by George Graham in 1737 and first executed by the clockmaker John Harrison in 1726.[232] Their dispute lead to a relatively bad-tempered exchange of a further seven papers at the Royal Society between Short and Ellicot in 1752 and 1753, in which their claims for priority, influence and originality were assessed in letters from, variously, E. Sparke (probably the clockmaker, Edward Sparke), John Harrison and the astronomer Nathaniel Bliss (FRS and Savillian Professor of Geometry at Oxford). Although these subsequent letters were not published in *Philosophical Transactions*, Birch was forced to notice the dispute in the Weekly Letter when Ellicot published a sixty-eight-page pamphlet in 1753 which comprised Ellicott's original paper, Short's 'Historical account' and nine replies and answers.[233] More damaging, Ellicott wrote a preface complaining that Short's attack was 'made with a View of injuring him in his profession & Business'. As Birch saw it, Ellicott's publication 'inform'd the public of his Dispute with Mr. Short', courting publicity that could bring the Royal Society into disrepute. Ellicott also attacked the Paper Committee for refusing to publish the vindications of his position, such as his own response to Short, or Sharpe's defence of his account. Birch noted these criticisms, but defended his actions:

---

[228] For an account of the science see Sorrenson, *Perfect mechanics*, pp. 110–19.

[229] Ellicott, 'Description and manner'.

[230] BL: Add MS 35398: Birch to Yorke, 6 June 1752, ff. 49–50 (50v).

[231] Royal Society: Journal Book Original: JBO/22 Thursday, 4 June 1752, 154–6. Ellicott, 'Description of two methods'.

[232] BL: Add MS 35398: Birch to Yorke, 1 September 1753, ff. 153–4; Short, 'Letter . . . concerning the inventor'.

[233] John Ellicott, *Description of two methods* (1753).

[T]he Committee of the Society's refusal to print Mr. Sparke's <u>Remarks</u> on Mr Short's <u>Hist. Account</u> as <u>in common justice might</u>, he says, <u>have been expected</u>. But he omits both the reason of that Refusal, which was the gross Indecency of the Reflections, & the Offer of publishing those Remarks when purg'd of the Invectives & supported by proper Authorities.[234]

Birch is concerned about Ellicott's public criticism of the new system of peer review: as Ellicott sees it, the Paper Committee had suppressed his freedom to respond, while Birch defended his actions as the preservation of civil and polite speech in scholarly debate. Birch returned to the topic in the Weekly Letter only because of Ellicott's pamphlet, which made public the dispute between fellows of the Royal Society. He is not interested in the science as much as the potential for institutional embarrassment, which he saw as an instrument of state power and cultural prestige.

Conclusion: Reading and the Royal Society

Birch and Yorke, as has been shown, were voracious and wide-ranging readers who used a well-organised and systematic correspondence to record their diverse reading encounters. They developed distinctive and studious reading practices to survey, identify, catalogue and summarise their reading while, at the same time, clearly seeing at least some reading matter as having an emotional appeal. The systematic aspects of their reading culture began with their own historical writing projects, from *Athenian Letters* through to *Memoirs of Queen Elizabeth*. These practices were subsequently deployed in processes that organised and categorised their reading of natural philosophy, especially learned journals and the publications of scientific institutions. So while the volume of reading events in the Weekly Letter points to the flood of knowledge in this period, as noticed by Ann Blair, it also points to how it could be managed and organised profitably.[235]

How distinctive was Birch and Yorke's reading? Drawing a comparison with other readers of a broadly similar station, it is clear that they are within the horizon of expectation, with regard both for the topics of their reading and for their reading practices. Useful comparisons can be made with other studies of individual readers from this period for whom substantial or quantitative analysis of their reading has been pursued: Thomas Reid, Elizabeth Montagu and Anna Larpent.[236] Figure 15 shows schematically the range of reading topics shown by these readers and compares them to the fare offered by

---

[234] BL: Add MS 35398: Birch to Yorke, 1 September 1753, ff. 153–4 (153v).

[235] Blair, *Too much to know*.

[236] Wood, 'Thomas Reid and the practices of reading'; Ellis, 'Reading practices in Elizabeth Montagu's epistolary network', p. 218; Brewer, 'Reconstructing the reader', p. 229.

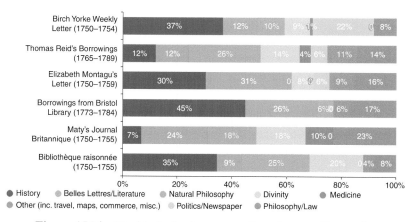

Figure 15 The Weekly Letter in comparative view: reading topics

relevant journals (Maty's *Journal Britannique* and Wetstein's *Bibliotheque Raisonée*) and, in a slightly different register, the borrowing records of the Bristol Library.[237] This chart is drawn from a variety of different research projects on reading among the educated and elite circles that compose or are adjacent to the republic of letters. As each uses analogous but different methods to categorise their reading topics, the chart has used a data-type normalisation process to indicate the relative significance of reading in history, *belles lettres* and polite literature, natural philosophy and learned journals, divinity, medicine, politics and newspapers and philosophy and law.

Thomas Reid (1710–96) was a professor of philosophy, first at the University of Aberdeen (1752–64) and then the University of Glasgow (1764–81). Paul Wood's analysis shows that Reid practised both silent individual reading (albeit often in a busy and noisy domestic situation) and collective oral reading, especially through sermons, lectures and papers delivered to scientific institutions. Reid's reading, which encompassed books, manuscript, pamphlets and ephemera, was sourced from his own library, but also, and significantly, from the institutional library of his university and from coffeehouses. Wood's research undertook a quantitative analysis of Reid's borrowings from the Glasgow University Library, as recorded in the 'Professors Receipt Book'. This shows he borrowed 615 books between 1767 and 1789, of which Wood is able to trace and classify 589. Reid's borrowings are composed of moral

---

[237] Janssens, *Maty and the* Journal Britannique, categories modernised by Janssens, pp. 66–7; Lagarrigue, *L'histoire externe de la 'Bibliothèque raisonnée'*, p. 190; Kaufman, *Borrowings from the Bristol Library.*

philosophy (11 per cent), natural philosophy (including natural history, mathematics and history) (19 per cent), learned journals (4 per cent) and theology (14 per cent). History (12 per cent) and polite literature (9 per cent) form an important but smaller part of his reading. Like Birch, Reid employed a series of note-taking practices to record his reading – extracts, remarks, abstracts and observations – using a format Wood argues is derived from Locke's 'New Method' of common-placing.[238] Analysing the books he abstracted, Wood found Reid most interested in natural philosophy (26 per cent), moral philosophy (25 per cent), mathematics (17 per cent) and natural history (9 per cent); which suggests studious habits of reading were reserved for science. Robert DeMaria's study of Johnson's reading does not take a quantitative approach, but the distinctions he makes between Johnson's modes of reading discussed in the Introduction, between study, perusal, mere reading and curious reading, have formative analogies with this research on Birch and Yorke.

A different comparison can be made by between Birch and Yorke's reading and that of two elite, well-educated women readers. Elizabeth Montagu was the central figure of the social reading circle of the Bluestockings, a coterie adjacent to the Hardwicke Circle. The evidence of Montagu's reading is recorded in her personal correspondence at the Huntington Library, San Marino (Montagu sent and received *c*.1,000 letters in the period 1750–9: compare the Weekly Letter, 139 letters 1750–4). An immediate finding is that Birch and Yorke's letters were more consistently interested in exchanging information about reading, books and manuscripts: while only 11 per cent of the Montagu letters discuss reading events, every Weekly Letter does. Analysis of the books and pamphlets identified in the Montagu circle letters (1750–9) that discussed their reading shows that 31 per cent were history; 36 per cent literature (13 per cent fiction, 4 per cent classics, 7 per cent drama, 9 per cent poetry, 3 per cent literary criticism), 9 per cent philosophy and 8 per cent divinity.[239] Compared to the Birch-Yorke circle, the Montagu circle was less interested in history, politics and news and natural history, and much more interested in literary and imaginative writing.

Another well-educated woman reader was Anna Larpent (1758–1832), the daughter of the diplomat Sir James Porter (FRS), who kept a diary for much of her life.[240] Larpent was married to John Larpent, a successful civil servant who held the post of inspector of plays in the Office of the Lord Chamberlain. Her

---

[238] Locke, 'A new method of a common-place-book', pp. 311–36. See Yeo, 'Locke, master note-taker', pp. 175–218.

[239] Ellis, 'Reading practices', p. 218.

[240] Anna Larpent, Diaries, 1773–1830, Huntington: HM 31201, 17 vols.

diary is not simply a record of her reading, but also records her extensive visits to the theatre, concerts and exhibitions of all kinds. John Brewer's analysis shows that, in the 1790s, she read more than 440 titles, including books, pamphlets, plays and sermons. Her reading interests incline more towards imaginative literature (51 per cent; novels (15 per cent), plays (17 per cent), classics (10 per cent), *belles lettres* (10 per cent) and poetry (2 per cent); history and biography (14 per cent) play a less pronounced role, as does natural philosophy (16 per cent). Brewer's analysis of Larpent's reading practices notes her confident critical judgement and her preference for women writers and works with female protagonists. She read many novels, but, like Birch, was critical of their moral influence, and of works that privileged emotional response. Larpent valued purposive, improving and didactic works; she distinguished 'between reading "in a followed manner" and more superficial perusal'; in the former mode, she wrote digests and abstracts of what she read.[241]

Comparison with these diverse readers demonstrates that Birch and Yorke's Weekly Letter is a project with distinctive features. As a newsletter reporting on knowledge networks in London, it generates a very large number of reading events, simply noting most and engaging more deeply with a smaller subset. The Weekly Letter adopts and refines reading practices associated with the studious work of learning and scholarship, such as summarising and abstracting, categorising and making critical judgements and attributions. Formally, the Weekly Letter functioned as a tool for information management, similar in some ways to the kinds of index or bibliography noted by Blair, that by surveying and categorising the flood of learning provided reference and finding devices.[242] The Weekly Letter was not a public resource, as Figure 7 shows: the letters were pasted into guard books, kept in 'the Wrest-Archives', as Yorke's study was called ironically.[243] Although the Weekly Letter was not itself public, it played a central role in the formation and influence of the Hardwicke Circle reading culture.

In this way, Birch and Yorke's reading practices illuminate their role and work in the Royal Society. As noted in Section 1, Da Costa suggested that the fellowship comprised two groups: the working members ('Physical') who actually performed scientific research, and the honorary members ('Nobility'), for whom fellowship allowed them to display their curiosity, patriotism and prestige.[244] Yorke was clearly an honorary member in this sense, and, while Birch was not in any sense of the Physical party, he was elected to the role of secretary for a scientific purpose: his ability and expertise

---

[241] Brewer, 'Reconstructing the reader', p. 240.   [242] Blair, *Too much to know*, pp. 117–72.
[243] BL: Add MS 4308: Jemima Lady Grey to Birch, Wrest, 25 July 1749, f. 205r.
[244] BL: Add MS 28535: Da Costa to William Borlase, 27 February 1752, f. 72r.

in scientific publishing, managing archival reforms and institutional administration. Especially under Macclesfield's presidency, Birch was given latitude to
reform *Philosophical Transactions* and the administrative machinery of the
Royal Society. To consolidate and enhance its reputation, both in Britain and
in Europe, Birch was contracted to write a new history of the Royal Society in
1754, the first since Thomas Sprat's in 1667. He began work in May 1754
making extracts from the Society's Journal Book.[245] As Birch declared in his
dedication to the king, the purpose was to reinforce the 'importance of
Experimental Philosophy and real Science to the interest of every Nation'.[246]
When the British Museum was founded in 1753, Yorke and Hardwicke were
among the principal trustees. Birch, subsequently an elected trustee, was called
in to the first meetings of the trustees to provide administrative expertise and
advice. As the analysis of their reading in the Weekly Letter suggests, Birch and
Yorke pivoted in the early 1750s from their first interest in early modern English
history, so typical of their Whig positioning, to the reform of a scientific
institution. By leveraging their curiosity about and facility with correspondence
and manuscripts, especially its management and archiving, they were able to
turn their reading habits to their programme, partly considered and partly
casual, to reform the working practices of the Royal Society and its
administration.

---

[245] BL: Add MS 4478C: Birch, Diary, 3 May 1754, f. 248r.
[246] Birch, *History of the Royal Society*, p. vi [iii].

Bibliography

Abbreviations for Manuscript References

BL   British Library, Department of Manuscripts, London
Huntington   Huntington Library, San Marino, CA
Lambeth   Lambeth Palace Library, London
Royal Society Royal Society Library, London

Weekly Letter Reading Database

The Weekly Letter Reading Database is available at:

www.cambridge.org/scienceandreading

Print

A bill, intituled, An act for regulating the commencement of the year; and for correcting the calendar now in use ([London, 1751]): 24 Geo.II.c.23.

A charge delivered to the Grand Jury, at the sessions of the peace held for the city and liberty of Westminster, on Wednesday the 16th of October, 1754 . . . to which is added, the presentment of the grand jury of the philosophical works of the late Right Honourable Henry St John, Lord Viscount Bolingbroke. Published by order of the court, and at the unanimous request of the gentlemen of the Grand Jury (London: printed for T. Payne, 1754).

A vindication of the free inquiry into the miraculous powers, which are supposed to have subsisted in the Christian church, &c. from the objections of Dr. Dodwell and Dr. Church (London: printed for R. Manby and H. S. Cox, 1751).

Allibone, Thomas Edward, *The Royal Society and its dining clubs* (Oxford: Pergamon, 1976).

Almagor, Yossi, 'Friendship in the shadow of patronage: the correspondence between Thomas Birch and Philip Yorke (1740–1766) revisited', *Erudition and the Republic of Letters* 4:4 (2019), 468–97.

Anderson, Douglas, '"Your most humble servant": the letters of Antony Van Leeuwenhoek', *FEMS Microbiology Letters* 369:1 (2022), 1–9.

Augier de Marigny, François, *Histoire des arabes sous le gouvernement des califes*, ed. by G. L. Calabre Perau. 4 vols. (Paris: chez la veuve Estienne et fils, 1750).

Bacon, Francis, *The works*, ed. by Basil Montagu. 12 vols. (London: William Pickering, 1830).

Banks, David, 'Thoughts on publishing the research article over the centuries', *Publications (Basel)* 6:1 (2018), 1–11.

Bannet, Eve Tavor, 'History of reading: the long eighteenth century', *Literature Compass* 10:2 (2013), 122–33.

Barre, Joseph, *Histoire générale d'Allemagne*. 11 vols. (Paris: Lespine and Herissant, 1748).

Beaumelle, Laurent Angliviel de La, and Voltaire, *Le siècle de Louis XIV. Nouvelle édition, augmentée d'un très grand nombre de remarques, par M. de La B*** [La Beaumelle]*. 3 vols. (Frankfort: Yve Knoch et J.G. Eslinger, 1753).

Berman, Jules J., *Principles of big data: preparing, sharing, and analyzing complex information* (Amsterdam: Elsevier, Morgan Kaufmann, 2013).

Besterman, Theodore, *Voltaire* (London: Longman, 1969).

Birch, Thomas, *A collection of the state papers of John Thurloe, Esq; secretary, first, to the Council of State, and afterwards to the two Protectors, Oliver and Richard Cromwell . . . containing authentic memorials of the English affairs from the year 1638, to the restoration of King Charles II. To which is prefixed, the life of Mr. Thurloe*. 7 vols. (London: printed for the executor of the late Mr. Fletcher Gyles, 1742).

Birch, Thomas, *The heads of illustrious persons of Great Britain, engraven by Mr. Houbraken, and Mr. Vertue*. 2 vols. (London: printed for John and Paul Knapton, 1743–51).

Birch, Thomas, *An historical view of the negotiations between the courts of England, France, and Brussels, from the year 1592 to 1617. Extracted chiefly from the MS. state-papers of Sir Thomas Edmondes, Knt.* (London: printed [by Samuel Richardson] for A. Millar, opposite to Katharine-Street, in the Strand, 1749).

Birch, Thomas, *The history of the Royal Society of London for Improving of Natural Knowledge, from its first rise*. 4 vols. (London: printed for A. Millar in the Strand, 1756–7).

Birch, Thomas, *The life of the Honourable Robert Boyle* (London: A. Millar, 1744).

Birch, Thomas, *Memoirs of the reign of Queen Elizabeth, from the year 1581 till her death. In which the secret intrigues of her court, and the conduct of her favourite, Robert Earl of Essex, both at home and abroad, are particularly illustrated. From the original papers of his intimate friend, Anthony Bacon, Esquire, and other manuscripts never before published*. 2 vols. (London: printed for A. Millar, 1754).

Blair, Ann, *Too much to know: managing scholarly information before the modern age* (New Haven, CT: Yale University Press, 2010).

Bolingbroke, Henry St John, Viscount, *Letters on the study and use of history* (London: printed for A. Millar, 1752).

Bolingbroke, Henry St John, Viscount, *The philosophical works of the late Right Honorable Henry St. John, Lord Viscount Bolingbroke*. 5 vols. (London: [s.n.] printed in the year 1754).

Bolingbroke, Henry St John, Viscount, *Reflections concerning innate moral principles* (London: printed for S. Bladon, 1752).

Bolingbroke, Henry St John, Viscount, *The works of the late Right Honorable Henry St. John, Lord Viscount Bolingbroke*. 5 vols. (London: printed in the year 1754).

Boyd, Danah, and Kate Crawford, 'Critical questions for big data: provocations for a cultural, technological, and scholarly phenomenon', *Information, Communication & Society* 15: 5 (2012), 662–79.

Boyle, earl of Orrery, John, *The letters of Pliny the Younger* (London: printed by James Bettenham, for Paul Vaillant, 1751).

Boyle, earl of Orrery, John, *Remarks on the life and writings of Dr. Jonathan Swift, Dean of St Patrick's, Dublin* (London: printed for A. Millar, 1752).

Brant, Clare, and George Rousseau (eds.), *Fame & fortune: Sir John Hill and London life in the 1750s* (London: Palgrave, 2017).

Brewer, John, 'Reconstructing the reader: prescriptions, texts and strategies in Anna Larpent's reading', in James Raven, Helen Small and Naomi Tadmor (eds.), *The practice and representation of reading in England* (Cambridge: Cambridge University Press, 1996), pp. 226–45.

Browne, Isaac Hawkins, *De animi immortalitate. Poema* (Londini: impensis J. & R. Tonson & S. Draper, 1754).

Browning, Reed, *Political and constitutional ideas of the court Whigs* (Baton Rouge: Louisiana State University Press, 1982).

Burditt, Paul F., 'The authorship of *The memoirs of Sir Charles Goodville* (1753)', *Notes and Queries*, 51:4 (2004), 406–7.

Burt, Ronald S., *Brokerage and closure: an introduction to social capital* (Oxford: Oxford University Press, 2005).

Carte, Thomas, *A general history of England* (London: printed for the author, 1747–55).

The Christian philosopher and politician (London: printed for W. Owen, 1750–1).

Clayton, Robert, *A vindication of the histories of the Old and New Testament. In answer to the objections of the late Lord Bolingbroke* ([London]: Dublin, printed, London, reprinted for W. Bowyer, and sold by M. Cooper and George Woodfall, 1752).

Compleat history of James Maclean, the gentleman highwayman, who was executed at Tyburn, on Wednesday Oct. 3. 1750 (London: printed for Charles Corbett, 1750).

Crebillon, Claude Prosper Jolyot de, *Catilina: tragédie en cinq actes, et en vers* (A Paris: Chez Prault fils, 1749).

D'Incarville, Pierre Nicolas Le Chéron, 'A letter from Father D'Incarville, of the Society of Jesus, at Peking in China', *Philosophical Transactions* 48 (1753–4), 253–60.

DeMaria Jr, Robert, *Samuel Johnson and the life of reading* (Baltimore, MD: Johns Hopkins University Press, 1997).

Des Maizeaux, Pierre (ed.), *Scaligerana, Thuana, Perroniana, Pithoeana, et Colomesiana*. 2 vols. (Amsterdam: Cóvens and Mortier, 1740).

Dobbs, Arthur, 'A letter . . . concerning bees, and their method of gathering wax and honey', *Philosophical Transactions* 46 (1750), 536–49.

Dodd, William, *A new book of the Dunciad: occasion'd by Mr. Warburton's new edition of the Dunciad complete* (London: printed for J. Payne and J. Bocquet, in Pater-Noster-Row, 1750).

Drucker, Johanna, *The digital humanities coursebook: an introduction to digital methods for research and scholarship* (London: Routledge, 2021).

Eaves, T. C. Duncan, and Ben D. Kimpel, *Samuel Richardson: a biography* (Oxford: Clarendon, 1971).

Ellicott, John. 'The description and manner of using an instrument for measuring the degrees of the expansion of metals by heat', *Philosophical Transactions* 39 (1736), 291–9.

Ellicott, John, *A description of two methods, by which the irregularities in the motion of a clock, arising from the influence of heat and cold upon the rod of the pendulum, may be prevented. . . . To which are added a collection of papers* (London: printed for R. Willock, 1753).

Ellicott, John, 'A description of two methods, by which the irregularity of the motion of a clock, arising from the influence of heat and cold upon the rod of the pendulum, may be prevented', *Philosophical Transactions* 47 (1751–2), 479–94.

Ellis, Markman 'Philip Yorke and Thomas Birch: scribal news in the mid-18th century', ed. Robin Eagles and Michael Shaich, *Parliamentary History* 41 (2022), 202–20.

Ellis, Markman, 'Reading practices in Elizabeth Montagu's epistolary network of the 1750s', in Elizabeth Eger (ed.), *Bluestockings displayed: portraiture, performance and patronage, 1730–1830* (Cambridge: Cambridge University Press, 2013), pp. 213–32.

Ellis, Markman, 'Thomas Birch's 'Weekly Letter' of 'Literary Intelligence' (1741–66): correspondence and history in the mid-eighteenth century Royal Society', *Notes and Records: The Royal Society Journal for the History of Science* 68: 3 (20 September 2014), 261–78.

Engelsing, Rolf, 'Die Perioden der Lesergeschichte in der Neuzeit', *Archiv für geschichte des Buchwesens* 10 (1970), 945–1002.

Fontenelle, Bernard Le Bovier de, *Théorie des tourbillons cartésiens*, ed. by C. Falconet (Paris: chez Hippolyte-Louis Guerin, 1752).

Formey, Jean-Henri-Samuel, *Mélanges philosophiques*. 2 vols. (Leide: Imprimerie d'Elie Luzac, 1753–4).

Garrick, David, *The poetical works of David Garrick, Esq.* (London: printed for George Kearsley, 1785).

Geikie, Archibald, *Annals of the Royal Society Club: the record of a London dining-club in the eighteenth & nineteenth centuries* (London: Macmillan and Company, 1917).

Goring, Paul, 'The elocutionary movement in Britain', in Michael J. MacDonald (ed.), *The Oxford handbook of rhetorical studies* (Oxford: Oxford University Press, 2017), pp. 559–68.

Gould, William, *An account of English ants* (London: printed for A. Millar, 1747).

Gunther, Albert Edward, *An introduction to the life of the Rev. Thomas Birch D. D., F.R.S., 1705–1766* (Halesworth: Halesworth Press, 1984).

Harris, P. R., *A history of the British Museum 1753–1973* (London: The British Library, 1998).

Higson, P. J. W., 'Hugh, Lord Willoughby of Parham: a neglected Society President', *The Antiquaries Journal* 52:01 (March 1972), 169–84.

Hill, John, *The adventures of Mr George Edwards, a Creole* (London: printed for T. Osborne, 1751).

Hill, John, *The adventures of Mr. Loveill, interspers'd with many real amours of the modern polite world* (London: printed for M. Cooper, 1750).

Hill, John, *A review of the works of the Royal Society of London* (London: printed for R. Griffiths, 1751).

Histoire de l'Academie royale des sciences et des belles lettres de Berlin (Berlin: Ambroise Haude, 1746–71).

Houston, Alan, 'Benjamin Franklin and the 'Wagon Affair' of 1755', *The William and Mary Quarterly* 66:2 (2009), 235–86.

Hubberstey, Jemima, 'The Wrest circle: literary coteries and their influence on landscape design, 1740–1760' (Oxford: unpublished DPhil thesis, 2022).

Hutcheson, Francis, *A system of moral philosophy* (Glasgow: R. and A. Foulis; London, A. Millar and T. Longman, 1755).

Janssens, Uta, *Matthieu Maty and the* Journal Britannique*, 1750–1755: A French view of English literature in the middle of the eighteenth century* (Amsterdam: Holland University Press, 1975).

Kaufman, Paul, *Borrowings from the Bristol Library, 1773–1784: a unique record of reading vogues* (Charlottesville: Bibliographical Society of the University of Virginia, 1960).

Kimber, Edward, *The life and adventures of Joe Thompson* (London: printed for John Hinton, 1750).

Klein, Lawrence, 'Gender, conversation and the public sphere in early eighteenth century England', in Judith Still and Michael Worton (eds.), *Textuality and sexuality: reading theories and practices* (Manchester: Manchester University Press, 1993), pp. 100–15.

Kleinman, Scott, 'Digital humanities projects with small and unusual data: some experiences from the trenches', 2016. http://scottkleinman.net/blog/2016/03/15/digital-humanities-projects-with-small-and-unusual-data.

La vie du Cardinal D'Amboise (Paris: Estienne Richer, 1631).

Lagarrigue, Bruno, 'Un temple de la culture européenne (1728–1753): L'histoire externe de la *Bibliothèque raisonnée des ouvrages des savants de l'Europe*' (Nijmegen: doctoral dissertation submitted to Katholieke Universiteit Nijmegen, 1993, rev. 2009).

Le Journal des Sçavans (Amsterdam [Paris], 1665–1792).

Leighton, C. D. A., 'The enlightened religion of Robert Clayton', *Studia Hibernica* 29 (1995), 157–84.

Levy, Michelle, and Betty Schellenberg, *How and why to do things with eighteenth-century manuscripts* (Cambridge: Cambridge University Press, 2021).

Locke, John, 'A new method of a common-place-book', in *Posthumous works of John Locke* (London: W. B. for A. J. Churchill, 1706), pp. 311–36.

Lyons, Henry George, 'The officers of the Society (1662–1860)', *Notes and Records of the Royal Society of London* 3:1 (1940), 116–40.

Macclesfield, George, 'Remarks upon the solar and the lunar years', *Philosophical Transactions* 46 (1749–50), 417–34.

Mairan, Jean-Jacques Dortous de, *Traité physique et historique de l'aurore boréale* (Paris: De L'Imprimerie Royale, 1754).

Mallet, David, *Memoirs of the life and ministerial conduct, with some free remarks on the political writings, of the late Lord Visc. Bolingbroke* (London: printed for R. Baldwin, at the Rose, in Pater-Noster-Row, 1752).

Marsak, Leonard, 'Cartesianism in Fontenelle and French Science, 1686–1752', *Isis* 50:1 (1959), 51–60.

Memoirs Sir Charles Goodville and his family: in a series of letters to a friend (London: printed for Daniel Browne, and J. Whiston, and B. White, 1753).

Middleton, Conyers, *An examination of the Lord Bishop of London's discourses concerning the use and intent of prophecy* (London: printed for R. Manby and H. S. Cox, 1750).

Miller, David, 'The "Hardwicke Circle": the Whig supremacy and its demise in the 18th-century Royal Society', *Notes and Records of the Royal Society* 52 (1998), 73–91.

Miller, David, '"Into the Valley of Darkness": Reflections on the Royal Society in the eighteenth century', *History of Science* 27:2 (1989), 155–66.

Miller, David, 'Thomas Birch (1705–1766), compiler of histories and biographer', in *Oxford dictionary of national biography* (Oxford, 2004). www.oxforddnb.com.

Montesquieu, Charles de Secondat, baron de, *De l'esprit des lois* (A Geneve: Chez Barillot, & fils [1748]).

Moureau, François, *Répertoire des nouvelles à main: dictionnaire de la presse manuscrite clandestine, XVIe–XVIIIe siècle* (Oxford: Voltaire Foundation, 1999).

Moxham, Noah, and Aileen Fyfe, 'The Royal Society and the prehistory of peer review, 1665–1965', *The Historical Journal* 61:4 (2018), 863–89.

Moxham, Noah, Anna Gielas and Aileen Fyfe, '"Accoucheur of literature": Joseph Banks and the *Philosophical Transactions*, 1778–1820', *Centaurus* 62:1 (2020), 21–37.

Mullini, Roberta, 'Reading aloud in Britain in the second half of the eighteenth century: theories and beyond', *Journal of Early Modern Studies* 7 (2018), 157–76.

Nadel, George H. 'New light on Bolingbroke's letters on history,' *Journal of the History of Ideas* 23:4 (1962), 550–7.

Naunton, Robert, *Fragmenta regalia, or Observations on the late Queen Elizabeth, her times and favorits* ([London]: Printed, anno Dom. 1641).

Nicholas, Donald, *Mr Secretary Nicholas, 1593–1669: his life and letters* (London: Bodley Head, 1955).

Nicholas, Edward, *The Nicholas papers*, ed. G. F. Warner. 4 vols. (Camden Society, new ser., 40, 50, 57, 3rd ser., 31, 1886–1920).

Nipps, Karen, 'Cum privilegio: licensing of the Press Act of 1662', *The Library Quarterly (Chicago)* 84:4 (2014), 494–500.

Nouvelle bibliothèque Germanique, ou histoire litteraire de L'Allemagne, de la Suisse, & des pays du Nord, 6 (1750), parts 2 (April–June) and 3 (July–September).

'Occasional prologue', *Whitehall Evening Post or London Intelligencer*, 22 September 1750.

Pearson, Roger, *Voltaire almighty: a life in pursuit of freedom* (London: Bloomsbury, 2005).

Pope, Alexander, *The Dunciad, complete in four books, according to Mr. Pope's last improvements. With notes variorum*, ed. William Warburton (London: printed for J. and P. Knapton in Ludgate-Street, 1749).

Pope, Alexander, *An essay on criticism. With notes by Mr. Warburton*, ed. William Warburton (London: printed for Henry Lintot, 1749).

Price, Leah, *How to do things with books in Victorian Britain* (Princeton, NJ: Princeton University Press, 2012).

Price, Leah, 'Reading: the state of the discipline', *Book History* 7 (2004), 303–20.

Raynal, Guillaume Thomas François, *Mémoires historiques, militaires et politiques de l'Europe*. 3 vols. (Amsterdam: Arkslée et Merkus, 1754).

Réaumur, René Antoine Ferchault de, *Mémoires pour servir à l'histoire des insects*. 6 vols. (Amsterdam, 1734–42).

Richardson, Samuel, *An address to the public, on the treatment which the editor of the history of Sir Charles Grandison has met with from certain booksellers and printers in Dublin* (London: printed [by Samuel Richardson] in the year, 1754).

Richardson, Samuel, *The history of Sir Charles Grandison*. 7 vols. (London: S. Richardson, 1753–4).

Roe, Thomas, Sir, *The negotiations of Sir Thomas Roe, in his embassy to the Ottoman Porte, from the year 1621 to 1628 inclusive* (London: printed by Samuel Richardson, at the expence of the Society for the Encouragement of Learning, 1740).

Roos, Anna Marie, *Martin Folkes (1690–1754): Newtonian, antiquary, connoisseur* (Oxford: Oxford University Press, 2021).

Sale, William Merritt, *Samuel Richardson: master printer* (Ithaca, NY: Cornell University Press, 1950).

Schaffer, Simon, Lissa Roberts, Kapil Raj and James Delbourgo, *The brokered world: go-betweens and global intelligence, 1770–1820* (Sagamore Beach, MA: Science History Publications, 2009).

Schellenberg, Betty, *Literary coteries and the making of modern print culture: 1740–1790* (Cambridge: Cambridge University Press, 2016).

Settle, Elkanah, *Augusta lacrimans. A funeral poem to the memory of the Honourable Sir Daniel Wray, Kt.* (London: printed for the author, 1719).

Shank, J. B., *The Newton wars and the beginning of the French Enlightenment* (Chicago, IL: University of Chicago Press, 2008).

Shebbeare, John, *The marriage act: a novel* (London: printed for J. Hodges; and B. Collins at Salisbury, 1754).

Short, James, 'A Letter … concerning the inventor of the contrivance in the pendulum of a clock, to prevent the irregularities of its motion by heat and cold', *Philosophical Transactions* 47 (1751–2), 517–24.

Smollett, Tobias, *The adventures of Ferdinand Count Fathom* (London: printed for T. Johnson, 1753).

Smollett, Tobias, *The adventures of Peregrine Pickle* (London: printed for the author: and sold by D. Wilson, 1751).

Sorrenson, Richard John, *Perfect mechanics: instrument makers at the Royal Society of London in the eighteenth century* (Boston, MA: Docent Press, 2013).

Spedding, Patrick, *A bibliography of Eliza Haywood* (London: Pickering & Chatto, 2004).

Strype, John, *The life of the learned Sir John Cheke, Kt. First instructer, afterwards Secretary of State to King Edward VI.* (London: printed for John Wyat, 1705).

Stukeley, William, *The correspondence of William Stukeley and Maurice Johnson, 1714–54*, ed. by Diana Honeybone and Michael Honeybone (Woodbridge: Boydell Press, 2014).

Supplement to Mr. Chambers's Cyclopædia: or, Universal dictionary of arts and sciences, ed. by George Lewis Scott (London: printed for W. Innys and J. Richardson, R. Ware, J. and P. Knapton, T. Osborne, S. Birt [and 10 others in London], 1753).

The tatler revived (London, 13 March to 15 September 1750).

Thompson, Lynda, *The scandalous memoirists: Constantia Phillips, Laetitia Pilkington and the shame of 'publick fame'* (Manchester: Manchester University Press, 2000).

Thomson, Thomas, *History of the Royal Society, from its institution to the end of the eighteenth century* (London: Robert Baldwin, 1812).

Toll, Frederick, *Some remarks upon Mr. Church's vindication of miraculous powders, &c* (London: Printed for J. Shuckburgh, 1750).

Voltaire, *Babouc; or, The world as it goes. To which are added, letters concerning his disgrace at the Prussian court: with his letter to his niece on that occasion* (London: printed for, and sold by W. Owen, 1754).

Voltaire, 'Epître de Monsieur de Voltaire au Cardinal Quirini' [dated 12 December 1751], *Oeuvres de Mr. de Voltaire* (A Dresden: Chez George Conrad Walther Libraire du roi, 1748–54), III (1752), 219.

Voltaire, *Epître au roi de Prusse* [1751], in *Œuvres complètes de Voltaire*, éd. Louis Moland. Vol. 10 (Paris: Garnier, 1877–85), pp. 360–2.

Voltaire, *La Mérope françoise ... avec quelques petites piéces de littérature* (Paris: Prault fils, 1744).

Voltaire, *Oeuvres de Mr. de Voltaire* (A Dresden: Chez George Conrad Walther Libraire du roi, 1748–54).

Voltaire, *Rome sauvée: tragedie* (A Berlin: Chez Étienne de Bourdeaux, 1752).

Voltaire, *Le siècle de Louis XIV.* 2 vols. (Berlin: Publié par M. de Francheville, 1751); trans as *The Age of Lewis XIV.* 2 vols. (London: R. Dodsley, 1752).

Voltaire, *Zayre: tragedie* (A Amsterdam: Chez Etienne Ledet, 1733).

Walpole, Horace, *Yale edition of Horace Walpole's correspondence.* 48 vols. (New Haven, CT: Yale University Press, 1960).

Warburton, William, *A view of Lord Bolingbroke's philosophy* (London: printed for John and Paul Knapton, 1754).

Warburton, William, *A view of Lord Bolingbroke's philosophy: in four letters.* 3 vols. (London, 1754, 1755).

Warner, William Beatty, *Licensing entertainment: the elevation of novel reading in Britain, 1684–1750* (Berkeley: University of California Press, 1998).

West, Gilbert, *Education, a poem: in two cantos. Written in imitation of the style and manner of Spenser's* Fairy Queen (London: printed for R. Dodsley, 1751).

Williams, Abigail, *The social life of books* (New Haven, CT: Yale University Press, 2017).

Wittmann, Reinhard, 'Was there a reading revolution at the end of the eighteenth century?' in Guglielmo Cavallo and Roger Chartier (eds.), *A history of reading in the West* (Amherst: University of Massachusetts Press, 1999), 284–312.

Womersley, David, 'Lord Bolingbroke and eighteenth-century historiography', *The Eighteenth Century* 28:3 (1987), 217–34.

Wood, Paul, 'A virtuoso reader: Thomas Reid and the practices of reading in eighteenth-century Scotland', *Journal of Scottish Thought* 4 (2011), 33–74.

The world. By Adam Fitz-Adam (London: printed for R[obert]. Dodsley in Pall-Mall, 1753–6).

Yeo, Richard, *Notebooks, English virtuosi and early modern science* (Chicago: University of Chicago Press, 2014).

Yorke, Philip, 'On the *Acta Diurna* of the *Old Romans*', *Gentleman's Magazine* X, 1740, Preface, pp. iii–viii.

Yorke, Philip, Charles Yorke (and eight others), *Athenian letters: or, The epistolary correspondence of an agent of the king of Persia, residing at Athens during the Peloponnesian war*. 4 vols. (London: printed by James Bettenham, [1741–3]).

Acknowledgements

I have benefitted from the advice and guidance of many people in completing this research. In particular I would like to thank Ruth Ahnert, Tamara Atkin, Warren Boutcher, Tita Chico, Mark Currie, Peter de Bolla, Richard Hamblyn, Suzanne Hobson, Guy Marriage, Stephanie Howard-Smith, Christopher Reid, Matthew Rubery, Betty Schellenberg, Adam Smyth, Bev Stewart, Tessa Thompson, Abigail Williams and Clair Wills. I would like to thank my colleagues at Queen Mary University of London and the staff of the British Library, the Royal Society Library and the Bodleian Library, as well as the Alexander Turnbull Library at Te Puna Mātauranga o Aotearoa. My family have also given unconditional support for the project, especially Sharon Ellis, Stead Ellis and Briony Ellis. I am very grateful to those who were able to give me their advice and criticism about the manuscript, especially Rebecca Beasley, Richard Coulton, Sam Halliday, Matthew Mauger, Scott McCracken and Miles Ogborn. At Cambridge University Press I would like to express my gratitude to Eve Tavor Bannet, Bethany Thomas, Adam Hooper and the two anonymous readers. Finally, I am most especially thankful for Rebecca Beasley's kindness and love, without which this project would not have prospered.

Cambridge Elements ☰

Eighteenth-Century Connections

About the Series
Exploring connections between verbal and visual texts and the people, networks, cultures and places that engendered and enjoyed them during the long Eighteenth Century, this innovative series also examines the period's uses of oral, written and visual media, and experiments with the digital platform to facilitate communication of original scholarship with both colleagues and students.

Cambridge Elements ≡

Eighteenth-Century Connections

Printed in the United States
by Baker & Taylor Publisher Services